BORN TO FIGHT:
Prison to Palace

REUEL MEBUIN, PhD, CRA

authorHOUSE®

AuthorHouse™
1663 Liberty Drive
Bloomington, IN 47403
www.authorhouse.com
Phone: 833-262-8899

Published by AuthorHouse 04/26/2021

ISBN: 978-1-6655-2177-2 (sc)
ISBN: 978-1-6655-2178-9 (hc)
ISBN: 978-1-6655-2179-6 (e)

Library of Congress Control Number: 2021908770

Print information available on the last page.

Any people depicted in stock imagery provided by Getty Images are models, and such images are being used for illustrative purposes only. Certain stock imagery © Getty Images.

This book is printed on acid-free paper.

Contents

Preface

"If you can't go back to your mother's womb, you'd better learn to be a good fighter." Anchee Min

When you got out of bed this morning, you were either faced with decisions or conflicts like; what to wear, which car to drive, what perfume to put on, and what to eat for breakfast etc. While these decisions or conflicts can seem obvious, they can get a little complicated when others are involved. For example, telling your teenage child to eat a meal of your choice but he or she would rather have something else or telling your child to dress a certain way but they would rather make their own clothing decisions. These conflicts can easily escalate to battles or fights, for example, when dealing with a life threatening health issue, divorce, bankruptcy, a cheating spouse, a nagging boss, financial issues, academic issues, relational matters, just to name a few. This goes to speak to the fact that we are constantly at war or in a battlefield. The Chinese-American writer, Anchee Min, recognized the fact that we are incessantly fighting and stated that we be prepared not only to fight but to be good fighters. The fact that we are continually fighting is also affirmed by Napoleon Hill and Julien Smith who respectively stated that, "Victory is always possible for the person who refuses to stop fighting" and "you will never be entirely comfortable. This is the truth behind the champion-he is always fighting something. To do otherwise is to settle."

The battles can be internal or external. We face them the minute we are born into this world. Battles have become a normal part of our daily living. We face them the minute we wake up in the morning up to the time we fall asleep at night. These battles can be brought on by our own doing (internal forces) or they can be brought on by circumstances or people beyond our control (external forces). These battles can have far-reaching consequences. Whatever the source, their magnitude or their consequences, the reality is that these battles are there and we will have to face them at some of point in life if we are not already facing them now.

Mighty and everlasting Father, I lift the one reading this book. I pray he or she may find it worth their time and may they be transformed by the reading of this book. May You, oh LORD, turn their misery into a message, their disappointment into a Divine appointment, their fears into faith; their sadness into gladness etc. Fill and strengthen them with the power to fight their daily battles. In their weakness, grant them Your strength. May You be glorified in and through their battles in Jesus Mighty Name. Amen

Chapter One

WE ARE CONSTANTLY AT WAR

"Now the Philistines gathered their armies together to battle, and were gathered at Sochoh, which *belongs* to Judah; they encamped between Sochoh and Azekah, in Ephes Dammim" 1ˢᵗ Samuel 17:1, NKJV

"I have been up against tough competition all my life. I wouldn't know how to get along without it." Walt Disney. What an honest assessment coming from one of this world's most successful business men who won 22 Academy Awards during his life time and was the founder of Disneyland and Walt Disney World theme parks. Many of us may not realize that we are always up against something, the truth is, we are constantly at war with the world. That is why the Bible says, "from the days of John the Baptist until now, the Kingdom of heaven has been subjected to violence and violent people have been raiding it." Matt 11:12, NIV. We are constantly at war or better still there is a war constantly going on in our lives. That is the reality of living in this dark and pessimistic world. However, many of us, if given the choice, will without a doubt, choose to not engage in any fight. But that will be living in a world of fantasy for we are constantly at war with the things that life throws at us. When a child is born into this world, one will think or expect that the child will come out singing praises for being liberated from the confines of "prison" (the mother's womb). Rather, most children come out crying as if to signal that they are fully aware of the battles and troubles that lie ahead. They probably may be signaling that they would rather stay in the confines of the prison cells of their mother's womb than face the ongoing battles of this world. They come out with their head as if to signal that they have to make quick thinking and decisions as to where they should "land." They come out with their head that embodies their eyes to survey the battles and their mouths ready to scare off any aggressors. The NLT makes the certainty of a battle very clear by stating that "even when I walk through the darkest valley..." Psalm 23:4, The word "when" signals a certainty that we will be faced with some challenges at a given time in our lives. It may not be now but it is certain to happen. It can take on different forms and different magnitudes but it is surely going to happen at some point in our lives.

The enemy and its agents are persistently throwing things at us. This could be in the form of sickness, unemployment, marital or relationship issues, financial issues, death of a loved one just to name a few. At creation, God desired the best for us. He created us in His image, for His likeness. He made us a little lower than the angels and crowned us with glory and honor; He made us rulers over the works of His hands and placed everything on earth under our feet (Psalm 8:5-6). But the enemy was not going to see us enjoy this glory. That is why in his schemes, he lured us away through sin. Since that fall in the Garden, life has been nothing but a fight.

While our challenges are many, we should keep up the fight for "the righteous person may have many troubles, but the LORD delivers him / her from them all" Psalm 34:19 NIV We are always fighting against unseen and spiritual forces "For our struggle is not against flesh and blood, but against the rulers, against the authorities, against the powers of this dark world and against the spiritual forces of evil in the heavenly realms" Ephesians 6:12 NIV. And in order to fight this battle, we must "…be strong in the Lord and in His mighty power. [11] Put on the full armor of God, so that you can take your stand against the devil's schemes…putting on the full armor of God, so that when the day of evil comes, you may be able to stand your ground, and after you have done everything, to stand. [14] Stand firm then, with the belt of truth buckled around your waist, with the breastplate of righteousness in place, [15] and with your feet fitted with the readiness that comes from the gospel of peace. [16] In addition to all this, take up the shield of faith, with which you can extinguish all the flaming arrows of the evil one. [17] Take the helmet of salvation and the sword of the Spirit, which is the word of God. [18] And pray in the Spirit on all occasions with all kinds of prayers and requests. With this in mind, be alert and always keep on praying for all the Lord's people. Ephesians 6:10-11, 13-18 NIV. Finally, we must know that our battles are temporal and are achieving for us an eternal glory that far outweighs all our troubles. 2nd Corinthians 4:17. When God called us, He did not promise us a trouble-free and/ or fight free life but instead, He promised us to be strong knowing that we will face battles or challenges. But when we do face these challenges, we should remember that He (God) will never forsake us nor abandon us (ref. Hebrew 13:5; Joshua 1:5,9; Deuteronomy 31:6, 8; Ps 94:14) and that He is bigger than the fights the devil will throw at us. Recall also that, Christ has already overcome the world (John 16:33). The devil had his opportunity to overcome while in heaven but he failed. He had another opportunity at the cross and he failed again. He was presented with one more opportunity at the grave (his own territory) and he failed again. Fighting battles is a surety in our lives and the Psalmist knows that he is constantly at war and took time to thank God for training his hands to fight stating "Praise be to the LORD my Rock, who trains my hands for war, my fingers for battle." Psalms 144:1 NIV. Fighting against the enemy is here to stay until the day we come face to face with our LORD and Savior.

Our daily fights come in various forms and moments. I am not sure how and when your fights have been, but as for me the fight took on different dimensions including but not limited to an arrest and detention by immigration and customs enforcement agents. This was going to prove as one of my biggest fights in my life. I was abruptly taken away from society with no advance notice, depriving me from a son and all the worldly things I amassed. I went on to serve 23 months and 3 weeks fighting the system under horrible inhuman conditions in three different detention centers in three different states. During this time, I was subjected to eating food that was spiced with roaches, rocks and many unwanted agents. I received the worst medical care one can think of as I spent 17 months in an enclosed facility during which about 16 hours of the day were spent in a small cell with another inmate. The cell was made up of a bunk bed, a reading stand and a toilet. Many times we were forced to eat in the cells; count it a blessing if you had a cellmate who was understanding enough to respect you, but when nature calls came and you had to release human waste, respect and understanding on the part of the one who needed to go was out of this world. During these times, I witnessed people develop serious mental breakdowns and many developed serious health situations. It became not a matter of "if" but "when" will I be next.

I do not know what battle you are engaged in right now. You may be dealing with serious health issues. You may be dealing with relationship issues. You may have lost your job, a loved one. You may be dealing with aging situation. You may be scrapping by just to make ends meet; to put food on the table for the family or to put a roof over your family. Whatever the situation you are facing, if this may sound as a conciliation, know that you are not alone. Even Christ who was Himself God, faced a fight in this dark world. After voluntarily stepping down from His throne of grace to come into this dark world to deliver us, we rejected Him. We despised Him. We insulted Him, we beat Him. We nailed Him (or crucified Him) to the cross and left Him there to bleed to death. The enemy did everything to want to stop Christ from delivering us. The enemy engaged our God in a fight that began from the day our Lord stepped into this world. But He did not quit. He did not give up. He did not fall prey to the enticement of the enemy. He lived in the world but was not of the world. He overcame the world. He conquered it. So brethren, let's take a clue from Christ, the author and finisher of our faith and fight on. Do not quit the battle. Christ did not quit? Why? Because he considered the joy set before Him and endured as stated in Hebrew 12:1-3 NIV "Therefore we also, since we are surrounded by so great a cloud of witnesses, let us lay aside every weight, and the sin which so easily ensnares *us,* and let us run with endurance the race that is set before us, looking unto Jesus, the author and finisher of *our* faith, who for the joy that was set before Him endured the cross, despising the shame, and has sat down at the right hand of the throne of God"

Some may see the word fight from a negative perspective and be tempted to question why I am encouraging everyone especially the believer or Christian to fight. No, the word is not presented from that negative perspective. Instead if any encouragement, it will be to pick and choose our fights and of course those fights will be the good fights worth fighting for. My focus here is letting you know that in this world, you will be engaged in a fight whether you like it or not. Having that advance knowledge can help better prepare you mentally, physically and spiritually on how to deal with them and which you should pick and engage in. Should you choose not to fight at all, you will fall for anything to reference the likes of Alexander Hamilton and Peter Marshall who once remarked that "if you don't stand for something, you will fall for anything." As you should know, it is not every fight that we must engage in. We must pick and choose the battles we must fight as there are certain things worth fighting for. As Paul encourages us in 1st Timothy 6:12 NKJV, "Fight the good fight of faith, lay hold on eternal life, to which you were also called and have confessed the good confession in the presence of many witnesses." He talks of the "good fight" because some fights are not fighting for. Such fights will qualify as bad fights and will include fighting with a spouse, fighting with others, fighting for the sole purpose of winning and not learning just to name these few.

Some of the fights worth fighting for include.

1) Your salvation (Philippians 2:12 NKJV "Therefore, my beloved, as you have always obeyed, not as in my presence

only, but now much more in my absence, work out your own salvation with fear and trembling")

2) To overcome (fleshly) worldly desires

The minute you become a believer by accepting Jesus Christ as your personal Lord and Savior, the battle against you just intensifies. That is why we are cautioned to be alert and of sober mind because our enemy the devil is always prowling around like a roaring lion looking for someone to devour (1st Peter 5:8). I can tell you the devil is not prowling around for everyone to devour but for a select group of people. He is definitely not attacking or devouring those in the world because he already owns them and he is certainly not attempting to devour those that are well grounded in the Word because they are guarded, protected and shield by the Precious Blood of the Lamb. He is certainly devouring the lukewarm Christian or the one that is weak in the Word or LORD. Once we are saved, the devil is not happy at all and will throw all sorts of schemes from his master book at us to try to gain us back. Though salvation is a free gift from God, we are to fight for it on a daily basis once saved. That is why we are told to fight the good fight of faith, to take hold of the eternal life to which we have been called when we first made our good confessions in the presence of many witnesses (1st Tim 6:12). So you can tell that we are constantly fighting for our "salvation" after all we are better off fighting for something than living for nothing. The Psalmist knew that he is constantly at war and pleaded with God to contend with those who contend with him and fight against those who fight against him (Psalm 35:1). We should also fight to overcome our fleshly, or worldly desires or lust. The flesh is constantly at war with the Spirit as we are told "For the flesh desires what is contrary to the Spirit, and the Spirit what is contrary to the flesh. They are in conflict with each other, so that you are not to do whatever you want." Galatians 5:17 NIV As stated before, we are also constantly fighting against the challenges the enemy throws at us. But while our challenges are many, we should keep up the fight for "The righteous person may have many troubles, but the LORD delivers him from them all." Ps. 34:19 NIV. And finally, we are always fighting against unseen and spiritual forces "For our struggle is not against flesh and blood, but against the rulers, against the authorities, against the powers of this dark world and against the spiritual forces of evil in the heavenly realms" Ephesians 6:12 NIV.

Questions

1) What fights are you engaged in? List three battles that you think you are constantly at war with.
2) Do you realize that Christ is in the boat (fight) with you? Who are your partners in this battle?
3) Where are you putting your trust? How are you trusting the source or sources where you are putting your trust?

Can you list 3 to 5 minor battles you are constantly or currently battling?

1) _____
2) _____
3) _____
4) _____
5) _____

Can you list 3 to 5 major battles you are constantly or currently battling?

1) _____
2) _____
3) _____
4) _____
5) _____

Prayer

God of Abraham, Isaac, Jacob, and Elijah, the God that answers by fire. I pray that the one who is reading this book right now will be encouraged to fight on. I pray O Lord that you will strengthen him or her to give up. I declare and degree by the Blood of Jesus, that you will be a victor and not a victim, a conqueror and not the conquered for the glory of the Living God.

Chapter Two

PREPARING FOR A FIGHT

Now that we have established without a doubt that we are constantly in a fight of some sort, the zillion-dollar question is "how do we respond and react to these fights?" Our answers to this question is very critical to our daily living. Charles Swindoll is quoted as saying, "life is 10% of what happens to you and 90% of how you react to it." Wow! So you mean to tell me that my response and reaction to the things that happen in my life is by far more impactful or meaningful compared to the actual things that happen to me? If so, this brings to light the issue of control, which we so often battle with. I cannot control most of the things that happen to me but I can control how I respond and react to these things. As discussed in a chapter ahead, we do not chose the battles in which we are engaged but we can control how we respond and react to these battles. You can respond and react to these battles before, during and after the battles. In the few paragraphs to follow, I will discuss how we can respond and react to our battles before the battles. That is, our preparation before battles.

The Whole Armor of God

[10] Finally, my brethren, be strong in the Lord and in the power of His might. [11] Put on the whole armor of God, that you may be able to stand against the [b] wiles of the devil. [12] For we do not wrestle against flesh and blood, but against principalities, against powers, against the rulers of [c]the darkness of this age, against spiritual *hosts* of wickedness in the heavenly *places*. [13] Therefore take up the whole armor of God, that you may be able to withstand in the evil day, and having done all, to stand.

[14] Stand therefore, having girded your waist with truth, having put on the breastplate of righteousness, [15] and having shod your feet with the preparation of the gospel of peace; [16] above all, taking the shield of faith with which you will be able to quench all the fiery darts of the wicked one. [17] And take the helmet of salvation, and the sword of the Spirit, which is the word of God; [18] praying always with all prayer and supplication in the Spirit, being watchful to this end with all perseverance and supplication for all the saints— [19] and for me, that utterance may be given to me, that I may open my mouth boldly to make known the mystery of the gospel, [20] for which I am an ambassador in chains; that in it I may speak boldly, as I ought to speak. *Ephesians 6:10-20 KJV*

It is in the Book of Ephesians that we are made aware that we are up against other spirits and/ or forces. No other Book in the Bible refers to this claim as Ephesians does. Let's discuss this passage in detail and see how we can apply this to our lives.

The armor of God. In order to properly prepare for war, we are to put on the **whole** armor of God. We need every weapon to fight with it. You cannot go to a battle front or field with partial weapons and/ or improper equipments. You need the complete weapon if you want to be victorious. So why the whole armor of God? Because our battles are not against flesh and blood but against spiritual hosts of wickedness (Ephesians 6:12); our battles are battles are against sin and Satan. The armor of God is consisted of six things are listed in the verses above;

(i) **The Belt of Truth (Ephesians 6:14 NKJV).** "Stand therefore, having girded your waist with truth…" The Truth is the central piece of the armor of God. The Truth is the Word of God, which is opposed to the lies of Satan. Jesus who stated, "And you shall know the truth and the truth shall make you free" (John 8:32 NKJV) said this of Satan in John 8:44 NKJV, "You are of *your* father the devil, and the desires of your father you want to do. He was a murderer from the beginning, and does not stand in the truth, because there is no truth in him. When he speaks a lie, he speaks from his own *resources,* for he is a liar and the father of it." The Truth is Jesus Christ. In John 14:6 NKJV, "Jesus said to him, "I am the Way, the Truth, and the Life. No one comes to the Father except through Me." Without the Truth, we are defenseless against our enemy. The belt of Truth is very powerful and we need it around our waist always. We need to know the truth and to commit ourselves to that truth. The enemy on the other hand wants to distort the truth by making us believe that the truth is within us, in our experiences, in our intelligence, common sense, status, beauty, or that the truth comes from other sources like our friends, the media, careers, families etc. I cannot emphasize enough the importance of knowing the truth and committing / submitting to that Truth. It is only in so doing that we can aptly fight the battles that the enemy throws at us.

(ii) **The breastplate of righteousness (Ephesians 6:14 NKJV)...**" put on the breastplate of righteousness" Righteousness refers to doing what is right in the eyes of God; doing what God requires us to do. As we work on living a righteous life, let's make sure we are not victims of 'comparative righteousness' aka self-righteousness in which one can claim to be more righteous than others. We should not compare our righteousness against each other because God says, all have sinned (Romans 3:23) and that there is no one righteous (Romans 3:10-12; Ps 14:1-3; Ps 53:1-3; Eccl 7:20). Also, we should guard against 'inputted or justifying righteousness whereby we claim that since Christ who knew no sin but became sin for my sake paid the price of my sin. Since He already paid the price of my sin, I can go on living the way I see fit...the grace of God becoming my passport to living a sinful life. This is in effect questioning the command to 'put on'..."why do I have to put on the breastplate of righteousness if God has already done so for me? What we should do as children of God is to embrace "realized righteousness" which calls on us to put on new clothes, image, attitude etc. This requires us to thrive to live like Jesus Christ. To put on the breastplate of righteousness means to cloth ourselves with Jesus. Before God can deliver us from the destructive hands of the enemy, we must first and foremost want to be delivered. I once had a discussion with a close associate who was dealing with the sins of attitude (pride, anger and envy) and actions (drunkenness and adultery). I counseled him over a period of time. During our last session, I asked him if he wanted to give up these sins of attitude and action. After prepping him that I was going to ask him a close ended question which required a simple yes or no answer, I presented the question three times, "do you want to give up.....?" Each time, he responded with a liturgy of excuses, justification, explanations etc. Even in those many sentences, he did not clearly say he was going to give up the sin or not. In order to confront an issue, you must first of all acknowledge or identify that it is an issue. You can only overcome that which you are willing to confront.

(iii) **The shoes of the Gospel (Ephesians 6:15 NKJV)**..."and having shod your feet with the preparation of the gospel of peace." The shoe speaks to our protection, stability and mobility. Without a good and fitting shoe, these three things will be greatly compromised especially when engaged in a battlefield. This also speaks to our readiness and preparedness for battle which is founded or grounded on our knowledge of the gospel; the gospel of peace. This peace does not mean that there is the complete absence of battles in our lives. Rather it speaks of a deep rooted harmony in us with God knowing that

He is in the boat with us (mark 4:35-41; Matthew 8:23-27) and that He will never forsake (emotional) us nor abandon (physical) us (Joshua 1:5,9; Deut. 31:6; Heb. 13:5-6; 1st Kings 6:13; 8:57; Jeremiah 1:8). This is the peace that comes from the Prince of Peace and it surpasses all understandings (Phil 4:7). This is the Peace with God that we have as a result of the peace of God which He has given us through the Blood of Jesus and the Cross. We cannot have this peace with God without first going through His only begotten son, Jesus Christ, whom He freely gave (not of our own accord or doing less we boast) to us. We respond to the Peace of God by responding and reacting to the Word of God; the Word that was in the beginning, was with God and was God (John 1:1) and the Word that became flesh and dwell among us (John 1:14).

(iv) **The shield of Faith (Ephesians 6:16 NKJV)**…"above all, taking the shield of faith with which you will be able to quench all the fiery darts of the wicked one" Faith is a gift from God and it is determined by God; who He is and not your circumstance. Faith therefore is not something that comes from within us. It is the substance of things hoped for, the evidence of things not seen (Heb. 11:1) and without it, it is impossible to please God (Heb. 11:6). Faith grants us access to God through Jesus Christ for it is what we have in Christ. Faith does not necessarily control God or twist His hands or His Will. You also do not need more faith or a deeper faith to twist God's hands. It is not about the quantity of faith that matters; it is about faith itself and the object of faith. Many Christians are under the misconception that if they can believe hard enough, they can twist God's hands or get Him into action. Satan will use fear and discouragement to cast a doubt in us and therefore not have faith but remember "God has not given us a spirit of fear, but of power and of love and of a sound mind." (2nd Tim 1:7 NKJV). In order to actively live out your faith, you have to act on it for "faith without works is dead" (James 2:20 NKJV). This requires a complete trust in God regardless of what your eyes are seeing or what you are experiencing.

(v) **The Helmet of Salvation (Ephesians 6:17 NKJV)**..."And take the helmet of Salvation..." The helmet protects our heads and the head is perhaps one of the most critical parts of the body. The head houses our thoughts and mind. Our thoughts and all that goes on in our minds can radically shape our daily life experiences. For example when we are so certain that Jesus Christ died for our sins, once and for all, we will not be moved by the onslaught of Satan's deceptive schemes. When you are so certain and are willing to proclaim that you "have overcome them because He who is in you is greater than he who is the world," there is nothing the one in the world will do that can move you or shaken you. Salvation is a gift from God and not something we gained or earned by our own doing; "For by grace, you have been saved through faith and that not of yourselves, it the gift of God not of works lest anyone should boast." (Ephesians 2:8-9 NKJV). Salvation is not an exclusive event but it encompasses an event in the past as we are saved (Titus 3:4-5), the present as we are being saved (2nd Corinthians 2:15) and the future as we will be saved (Romans 5:9-10).

(vi) **The Sword of the Spirit (Ephesians 6:17 NKJV)**…"And take…the sword of the Spirit which is the Word of God." The Sword of the Spirit is clearly defined for us as the Word of God. The Sword of the Spirit is the only offensive weapon listed in the armor of God. The rest of the weapons are defensive in nature. The Word which is "living and powerful, and sharper than any two edged sword (Heb. 4:12) can also be used both defensively as in Ephesians 6:14 and offensively as used here in Ephesians 6:17. Jesus Himself used the Word when He came under attack by the enemy when He stated, "it is written…" (Mt 4:1-11; Lk 4:1-12). God's Word is the Truth (John 17:17) and it is a lamp to our feet and a light to our path (Psalm 119:105).

(vii)   **Prayer (Ephesians 6:18)**. Prayer is not actually part of the armor of God but it is important to note that prayer is a critical piece in fighting our battles. Prayer is very critical to bring us in communion and fellowship with our Almighty Father, the great Warrior and the owner of our battles (2nd Chronicles 20:15; 1 Samuel 17:47)

Relationship: What it takes!!! You may feel (or maybe feeling) very overwhelmed with the putting on of the armor of God but it is not as difficult as the enemy may make you feel. Putting on the armor of God is as easy as having a relationship with Jesus. God is all about a relationship, a personal relationship with Him grounded on a complete trust of Him and a complete surrender to Him of all that you are going through and granting Him total control to be in charge. Our God is a relational God (1st Peter 1:3-5; 1st Peter 5:6-7; 2nd Corinthians 5:17-18; Romans 5:1-5). In her early age of marriage, my mother was subjected to many afflictions brought upon by the enemy that she decided life was not worth living at all. I was just few months on earth and my mother thought it will be best to take both of our lives than live under the circumstances life or the enemy had thrown at her. While she was in the process of executing the planned act and because she already had a relationship with God, she decided to speak to God one more time before the final execution of such an abominable act. As she did this, she heard a voice (Holy Spirit) commanding her to stop such a horrible act. Due to her personal relationship with God, she decided to speak to Him one more time before taking away our lives, she was able to hear God speak to her. Because of this personal relationship, she and I have lived on to testify about this "painful" event.

There are a few dos and don'ts I should caution you (in brief) about to be aware of when you are in the battle field. Be yourself; resist the temptation to be someone else and refuse to use their experiences or their resources. Encourage yourself. Be courageous and be ready to confront your fears head-on. Note that whatever you cannot confront, you cannot overcome or conquer. Be responsible and do not listen to negative people. Do not pay much attention to rejections. While rejections may seem as distractors, they are actually an indication that you had been chosen by God for the occasion. They are rejecting you because God did not want you to fit in. He (God) does not want anyone to receive His glory when He exalts you. Do not give up. Always recall and testify about your past victories and remember to praise the LORD for those past victories.

1) How do you prepare for your battles in lives?

2) What weapons do you use in fighting your battles? Will you still use these weapons? Why or why not?

3) How do you use these weapons in your battles?

4) What are some of the outcomes you have experienced after using these weapons named in question 2 above?

List 3 to 5 ways in which you prepare for battles.

1) _____

2) _____

3) _____

4) _____

5) _____

List 3 to 5 Weapons you are utilizing or often utilize in your battles

1) _____

2) _____

3) _____

4) _____

5) _____

Chapter Three

WE DO NOT CHOOSE MOST
OF OUR BATTLES

**"Then Jesse said to his son David, "Take now
for your brothers an ephah of this dried *grain* and
these ten loaves, and run to your brothers at the
camp" 1ˢᵗ Samuel 17:17 NKJV**

The fact that we do not chose most of our battles may sound
contradictory to my statement in the first chapter where I call on
you to choose your battles wisely (1ˢᵗ Tim 6:12). The point here is
that most of the battles we find ourselves in are thrown at us with no
pre-meditation on our part. No one in his or her right mind wakes
up in the morning and decides that they will go about fighting
unless you are a Lucifer or his agent. We all desire good in life. We
all desire to see this world a better place, at least in our eyes. We may
not agree with what is good or how that good is defined. When God
created us, He gave us the ability and propensity to do good until
we sinned through the first Adam. Despite the sin nature inherent
in us, some of the battles we engage in at times may not be of our
making or choosing. Think of the financial crises that rocked the

global economy in recent memories. Some of us had very little or nothing to bring about such crises. Think of the recent outbreak of diseases, war, natural disaster. You and I may have done nothing to bring about these incidences but they came anyways. Think of the bystander who is shot down by a stray bullet. Think of the child who is stricken by a sickness or death and leaves the parents with their heads scratching. We can do all we can in our powers and abilities to prevent these battles but they are bound to come our way for as long as we live in this darken world.

When David got up from sleep this faithful day to go about minding his business of mending the family's animal, little did he know that a different assignment was in store for him. He had very little say in it. When he got up, his father, Jesse, told him to take some roasted grains and bread to his brothers who were engaged in a battle against the Philistines. His planned "To Do List" was altered without consultation. His planned path for the day was going to witness a detour.

Many times, we find ourselves in such a predicament. The question that remains that we should be asking ourselves is "what do you do when you find yourself in such a predicament?" We are not told that David protested his father or questioned God. So it will be very fair to assume that he went along with the plans. You see many at times, it makes every logical sense to not question certain things. When the enemy throws things at us, rather than ask God these questions; "WHY ME?" or "why He allowed this detour in the first place?", we should be seeking God's purpose in allowing those detours. Recall that the greatest "WHY" question was posed by Christ (Himself God) while on the Cross. The Bible tells us in Matthew 27:46 NIV that "About three in the afternoon Jesus cried out in a loud voice, "Eli, Eli, lema sabachthani?" (which means "My God, my God, why have You forsaken me?" Do you know what is so interesting, He never received an answer from God the Father! If He, being God, did not receive (in part because He was asking a rhetorical to which He already knew the answer and His divine purpose) why should I, a mere mortal human being, expect God to give me an answer?

Nothing takes our all-knowing God off guard. Nothing happens by chance, coincidence or accident. He allows it for us a purpose. When God was delivering the Israelites from Egypt, He instructed Moses to lead the Israelites to a different and seemingly treacherous path.

"Then the Lord said to Moses, "Tell the Israelites to turn back and encamp near Pi Hahiroth, between Migdol and the sea. They are to encamp by the sea, directly opposite Baal Zephon. ³ Pharaoh will think, 'The Israelites are wandering around the land in confusion, hemmed in by the desert.' Then I will harden Pharaoh's heart, so that he will pursue them; and I will gain honor over Pharaoh and over all his army, that the Egyptians may know that I *am* the LORD." So the Israelites did this." Exodus 14:1-4 NIV.

Also recall the story of Job. Many consider him to be the first priest and many consider the book of Job as the oldest Book. In his time, Job is said to faithfully obey God. He will often give offerings on behalf of his children fearing they may have committed some sins. Job was said to be the richest man on earth in his time. However, one day, with no prior warnings and reasons unknown to Job, his world will come falling apart. While Job could not fully grasp what was going on, the Bible tells us that God Himself allowed this:

One day the angels came to present themselves before the LORD, AND SATAN ALSO CAME WITH THEM. [7] The LORD SAID TO SATAN, "WHERE HAVE YOU COME FROM?" Satan answered the LORD, "FROM ROAMING THROUGHOUT THE EARTH, GOING BACK AND FORTH ON IT."

[8] Then the LORD SAID TO SATAN, "HAVE YOU CONSIDERED MY SERVANT JOB? THERE IS NO ONE ON EARTH LIKE HIM; HE IS BLAMELESS AND UPRIGHT, A MAN WHO FEARS GOD AND SHUNS EVIL." [9] "Does Job fear God for nothing?" Satan replied. [10] "Have you not put a hedge around him and his household and everything he has? You have blessed the work of his hands, so that his flocks and herds are spread throughout the land. [11] But now stretch out your hand and strike everything he has, and he will surely curse you to your face." [12] The LORD SAID TO SATAN, "VERY WELL, THEN, EVERYTHING HE HAS IS IN YOUR POWER, BUT ON THE MAN HIMSELF DO NOT LAY A FINGER."

THEN SATAN WENT OUT FROM THE PRESENCE OF THE LORD.

We find ourselves in this situation quite often. You get up in the morning ready to go about your daily routines and the enemy begins the attack. That is the world we live in. Things will come our way whether we like it or not. Things will happen to us whether we have caused it or not. When these things happen, it does not negate the fact that God is still in control. These happenings do not change who God is; the Sovereign and all-knowing king of kings. But when the things happen, our response or reaction to it can make the difference between life and death; success or failure. In David's case, he quietly obeyed the father. In Job's case, he lost all his wealth, his children, his health and even his wife but in all of these things, "Job got up and tore his robe and shaved his head. Then he fell to the ground in worship [21] and said: "Naked I came from my mother's womb, and naked I will depart. The LORD GAVE AND THE LORD HAS TAKEN AWAY; MAY THE NAME OF THE LORD BE PRAISED." In all this, Job did not sin by charging God with wrongdoing." Job 1:20-22 NIV

In March of the year of my greatest trial, I got up in the morning, and got ready to go about my daily business. I left the house first leaving my son in doors (I was a single parent then) to get my car that was parked behind the house. Normally when I pull up the car from the back yard, I park the car in the driveway waiting for it to warm up. While waiting for the car to warm up, my son and I will be in the car praying for a trouble-free day and committing our entire day's activities into the Hands of the LORD. That was our routine. As we sat in the car praying, I spotted two cars parked on the street each facing the opposite direction. I live near a university campus on a street where you can only park on one side of the street. I have seen police give out so many tickets to illegally parked cars on this street. Most of these illegally parked cars are by students who are either always in the rush to go to class or who out rightly fail to pay attention to the street signs. When I saw these cars, my first instincts were to blame these students who park cars without paying attention to street signs thereby incurring parking fees which are often paid for by their parents. After our prayer, I took this opportunity to have a teachable moment with my son cautioning him to always read street signs before he parks a car because it can be costly to park in the wrong spot. I also caution to always give himself ample time for his appointments so he will not find himself parking illegally because he had no time to read posted street signs. I did not know whether these two cars especially the one parked on the wrong side had occupants in it as it had semi tinted windows and it was a block and half away from my view. When I drove off, both cars started driving at the same time. The one which was wrongfully parked started driving behind me since I drove towards the direction it was facing. At this point, I guessed that the occupant of the car following me was communicating with the other driver via some communication device they had in the car. In all of this it did not make sense to me. I had nothing to be concerned about and I was particularly observant that the car following me was driving behind me all this while. The road to my first destination is not straight, many turns are involved. If I was a little street smart or had some concerns, I probably could have paid attention to the car following me to know that it was driving behind me. When I got to my son's school, I got out of the car to walk him across the street since I came through the opposite direction. Just at that time, this car made a 180 decree turn. I stood there in great alarm that someone would make such a turn in a school zone. I didn't realize that it was one of the cars I saw parked on my street. I was pulled over less than 5 minutes after driving off my son's school. I wondered whether I had my seat belt on or whether I had failed to put on my signal lights on as I made a turn unto the major road. I immediately started reaching out to my glove compartment to bring out my necessary car and insurance documents but the gentleman who was not in uniforms flashed his badge at me and told me not to worry about getting the documents. Note that this guy only stepped out of the car to talk to me when

25

the other car had pulled up to the front of my car blocking me. I was ordered out of the car and they introduced themselves to me. The conversation went something like this:

Agents: Hi, come out of the car. We are from ICE

Me: ICE (thinking of real ice)?

Agent: Yes, ICE as in immigration.

Me: Immigration? What do you want

Agent: We are here for you.

Me: Excuse me? Me!! You must be looking for the wrong person. I have nothing to do with ICE.

Agent: Yes, we are looking for you (at this time pulling out my Facebook cover picture)

I was a bit confused given that I had just applied for citizenship (naturalization) some few months ago. I had gone through the entire process and as a matter of fact, I was in the Federal Building barely two days ago to find out the status of my naturalization process. While at the Federal Building, I was told they were having a back log and the agent promised me then they would get to me as soon as possible. I stood very perplexed at all that was happening now. The arresting agents told me that I was under arrest and that they will explain to me when I get to the central or main office. I told them what I was up to and the things I had planned for the day including a trip to the doctor's office. They assured me that my visit to their office will be very brief. While this seemed a like a detour (perhaps a reason why I reacted in a nonchalant manner), it was a beginning of a detour that will forever change my life.

God has a way to knock us out of our routine. Often times when we leave the house to go about our daily lives, we encounter detours in our lives. Detours in our plans can come in minor situations like a tire leak, the bus running late, spilling coffee on our clothes etc. It could also come in major circumstances like sickness, the loss of a loved one, loss of a job, bankruptcy etc.

We will always experience detours in life. The question now is, what do you do when you encounter the detours? As Epictetus was once quoted as saying; "It's not what happens to you, but how you react to it that matters." Kenneth H. Blanchard is quoted as saying "We can't always control what happens in our lives- things will go well, things will go poorly-but what we can control is our response to those events." Finally, I agree with Charles R. Swindoll who is quoted as saying ""Life is 10% of what happens to you and 90% of how you react to it"

victories.

1) What are some of the detours you are experiencing in your life now?

2) How are you handling these detours?

3) What are some of the things you will do differently to avoid these detours?

4) How and what do you see God's role in your detours?

Can you list 3 to 5 minor detours you are currently encountering?

1) _____

2) _____

3) _____

4) _____

5) _____

Can you list 3 to 5 major detours you are currently faced with?

1) _____

2) _____

3) _____

4) _____

5) _____

Precious Father, my Lord and my God, help us oh LORD to recognize the detours that come into our lives and to respond to them accordingly. May You order my footsteps and keep it away from crooked paths. May I not walk in the counsel of the ungodly nor stand in the path of sinners nor sit in the sear of the scornful. But may I delight in Your Law, LORD and meditate in it day and night in Jesus Mighty Name. Amen.

Chapter Four

THE GOLIATHS WE FACE MAYBE INVINCIBLE AND/ OR INVISIBLE IN THE NATURAL REALM

"But David said to Saul, "Your servant used to keep his father's sheep, and when a lion or a bear came and took a lamb out of the flock, ³⁵ I went out after it and struck it, and delivered *the lamb* from its mouth; and when it arose against me, I caught *it* by its beard, and struck and killed it. ³⁶ Your servant has killed both lion and bear; and this uncircumcised Philistine will be like one of them, seeing he has defied the armies of the living God." ³⁷ Moreover David said, "The LORD, WHO DELIVERED ME FROM THE PAW OF THE LION AND FROM THE PAW OF THE BEAR, HE WILL DELIVER ME FROM THE HAND OF THIS PHILISTINE." And Saul said to David, "Go, and the LORD BE WITH YOU!" 1st Samuel 17:34-37 NKJV

At some point, we all face difficulties and challenges. If you have not, then I will want to exchange my life with yours. Even so I may be very reluctant to exchange my life with yours because you either maybe living in a fantasy (wishful) world or you are probably telling one of those biggest lies that ever existed. The challenges we face in our lives come in many forms or magnitude. They may be visible or invisible. They may be internal or external. They may also appear to be invincible, indomitable or unconquerable. When the Israelites were faced with Goliath, they were deeply afraid because they felt he was invincible:

> "And a champion went out from the camp of the Philistines, named Goliath, from Gath, whose height *was* six cubits and a span. ⁵ *He had* a bronze helmet on his head, and he *was* armed with a coat of mail, and the weight of the coat *was* five thousand shekels of bronze. ⁶ And *he had* bronze armor on his legs and a bronze javelin between his shoulders. ⁷ Now the staff of his spear *was* like a weaver's beam, and his iron spearhead *weighed* six hundred shekels; and a shield-bearer went before him. ⁸ Then he stood and cried out to the armies of Israel, and said to them, "Why have you come out to line up for battle? *Am* I not a Philistine, and you the servants of Saul? Choose a man for yourselves, and let him come down to me. ⁹ If he is able to fight with me and kill me, then we will be your servants. But if I prevail against him and kill him, then you shall be our servants and serve us." ¹⁰ And the Philistine said, "I defy the armies of Israel this day; give me a man, that we may fight together."

¹¹ When Saul and all Israel heard these words of the Philistine, they were dismayed and greatly afraid" 1ˢᵗ Sam 17:4-11 NKJV

Also recall the report that was presented to Moses by the spies Moses had sent to spy the land the God of the Universe had promised them? 10 of the 12 spies indicated that the land was occupied by gigantic giants who were too strong for them:

> Then they told him, and said: "We went to the land where you sent us. It truly flows with milk and honey, and this *is* its fruit. ²⁸ Nevertheless the people who dwell in the land *are* strong; the cities *are* fortified and very large; moreover we saw the descendants of Anak there. ²⁹ The Amalekites dwell in the land of the South; the Hittites, the Jebusites, and the Amorites dwell in the mountains; and the Canaanites dwell by the sea and along the banks of the Jordan...³¹ ...We are not able to go up against the people, for they *are* stronger than we." Numbers 13:27-29, 31 NKJV

While they agreed that the Promised Land was full of milk and honey, they concluded that the inhabitants were stronger and as such they (the Israelites) could not defeat them. They stated that they even saw the Anaks there. Who are these Anaks? Genesis 6:4 NKJV states "There were giants on the earth in those days, and also afterward, when the sons of God came in to the daughters of men and they bore children to them. Those were the mighty men who were of old, men of renown." The scriptures also state that these giants died out when God sent a worldwide flood to destroy "all flesh" upon the earth.

Since these giants were a natural genetic variation of human beings, they all died along with all that was on earth then with the exception of Noah and all that he had placed in the ark.

> "21 And all flesh died that moved on the earth: birds and cattle and beasts and every creeping thing that creeps on the earth, and every man. **22** All in whose nostrils was the breath of the spirit of life, all that was on the dry land, died. **23** So He destroyed all living things which were on the face of the ground: both man and cattle, creeping thing and bird of the air. They were destroyed from the earth. Only Noah and those who were with him in the ark remained alive." Genesis 7:21-23 NKJV

The Bible also talks of the 3 Jewish boys (Shadrach, Meshach and Abednego) who faced a goliath in the person of Nebuchadnezzar and the blazing furnace. Nebuchadnezzar had set up a golden image for himself. It was commanded "that at the time you hear the sound of the horn, flute, harp, lyre, and psaltery, in symphony with all kinds of music, you shall fall down and worship the gold image that King Nebuchadnezzar has set up; ⁶ and whoever does not fall down and worship shall be cast immediately into the midst of a burning fiery furnace." Daniel 3:5-6 NKJV. These young boys defied such orders and earned themselves a quick passport into the blazing furnace; a furnace that was heated 7 times hotter than a normal furnace. The heat of this furnace was so intense that it even consumed the lives of the soldiers that took up Shadrach, Meshach and Abednego to throw into the furnace.

Your goliaths can also be invisible. Many in our world today, suffer from some form of health, mental or emotional issues. Some of these issues maybe very devastating but yet invisible to many even ourselves. Many believers on a worship day put on the best clothes, perfume, deodorant etc. and come to church looking very good but behind those fine clothes, nice perfumes and smiley faces, it's a whole lot of a different ball game. I am not asking everyone to unmask their internal problems for the world to see or know but if you could just take a snapshot of what is going on in people's personal and internal lives, you will be amazed. I do not take lightly anyone suffering from any of these ailments but you will agree with me that the consequences or toll on one's life and even the lives of others can be very devastating.

Couple of years ago, when I embarked on a journey of normalizing my residency status here in the country (US), I faced the greatest goliath in my life at the time. I had an encounter with the representatives of US Immigration and Customs Enforcement (ICE); an encounter which will go on to change the trajectory of my life and/ or world forever. By the way for those who may not already know, the US may probably be the only country where an immigration (civil) related matter is treated worse than a criminal matter. What initially seemed to me like a joke turned out to be a stay in the "University of ICE" for 23 months and three weeks. Yes, it is true that I didn't have to worry about what to eat, where to sleep, what bills to pay etc. (just trying to make light of the situation) but the truth is, I was facing an invincible or indomitable goliath. During detention one was subjected to the worst verbal, emotional, mental and psychological abuse or torture you could ever think of at the hands of the correction officers, deportation officers and other

33

fellow detainees. Just imagine for a minute being locked in a cell for 16 to 18 hours on a normal day and when you are released out of this cell for the remaining 6 to 8 hours, you are still locked in an enclosed area with no source of fresh air and/ or sun light. Imagine being locked in this cell for about 23 and half hours in a 24-hour period. You take this scenario further and imagine yourself in this cell with a total stranger, a person whose hygiene, experience, goals, communication, culture etc. are completely different with yours. To make matters worse, this cell also houses your toilet and at any given time your cellmate has to use the toilet in your presence. The abuse or torture was particularly worst or noticeable at the hands of Deportation Officers who will spare nothing to accomplish their goal of deporting you. It was a battle that could either make or break one. You needed more than your "physical self" to fight a battle of this nature or magnitude.

Your attitude, belief, faith and conviction will help you overcome your Goliath(s). David depended on the LORD to successfully face his goliath. He stated, "...You come against me with sword and spear and javelin, but I come against you in the name of the Lord Almighty, the God of the armies of Israel..." 1st Samuel 17:45 NIV. Of the 12 spies, 2 (Joshua and Caleb) did not dispute or discount the others' report but they were confident that they will overcome the "giants." "Then Caleb quieted the people before Moses, and said, "Let us go up at once and take possession, for we are well able to overcome it." Numbers 13:30 NKJV. Joshua and Caleb knew that God was faithful to Himself and His name and will keep His promise. Shadrach, Meshach and Abenego also placed their conviction in God and replied to king Nebuchadnezzar stating "...O Nebuchadnezzar, we have no need to answer you in this matter. [17]

If that *is the case,* our God whom we serve is able to deliver us from the burning fiery furnace, and He will deliver *us* from your hand, O king. [18] But if not, let it be known to you, O king, that we do not serve your gods, nor will we worship the gold image which you have set up." Daniel 3:16-18 NKJV.

When it dawned on me that I will be in "University of ICE" for a while except I agree to give up the fight and be deported to a country where threats to my wellbeing, future and existence were eminent, it became very clear to me that I will have to depend on a higher authority. I was weak, tired, exhausted, and frail. The whole world seemed to collapse around me. I knew I had to depend on God like never before. I could only win this battle by staying in His Word and spending time on my knees. Anything shy of this was a sure path to deportation. I lost it all. I lost my "family" I lost my job and finances, I lost my relationships, I lost a lot of courage and strength. I lost a lot of time. However, I did not lose the faith. I did not lose the Bible. I did not lose the desire and/ or will to go on my knees. I knew my victory was going to come through faith and keeping the good fight not by crying, whining or questioning what was going on. I knew our God is not moved by tears but He is moved by faith, prayers and obedience.

The Bible narrates a battle between the Israelites and the Amalekites. We are told that as Moses held up his hand, the Israelites were winning but when he let down his hands, the Amalekites prevailed. Lifting his hand up signifies praying to God, seeking and depending on God. Moses did not count on the strength of the Israelites' army but they trusted God.

"And so it was, when Moses held up his hand, that Israel prevailed; and when he let down his hand, Amalek prevailed. ^{12} But Moses' hands *became* heavy; so they took a stone and put *it* under him, and he sat on it. And Aaron and Hur supported his hands, one on one side, and the other on the other side; and his hands were steady until the going down of the sun." Exodus 17:11-12 NKJV

Also recall when Nehemiah was rebuilding Jerusalem's wall. He depended so much on God and not their prowess. He kept his plans away from others and only revealed it at the appropriate time. When others injected negative thoughts, feelings, mockery and ridiculed them, Nehemiah depended on the God of the universe.

"^{19} But when Sanballat the Horonite, Tobiah the Ammonite official, and Geshem the Arab heard of it, they laughed at us and despised us, and said, "What *is* this thing that you are doing? Will you rebel against the king?" ^{20} So I answered them, and said to them, "The God of heaven Himself will prosper us; therefore we His servants will arise and build, but you have no heritage or right or memorial in Jerusalem." Nehemiah 2:19-20 NKJV

Seeking and trusting God always in all situations should be the proper attitude anyone should have while in a battle field. In doing so, you will surely come out victorious as those who put their trust in the LORD will not be put to shame (1st Peter 2:6; Isaiah 28:16, 49:23; Ps. 25:3; Romans 9:33, 10:10)

People wrote me off. Others said lots of things about me. Some gave me all sorts of labels. Others made all sorts of conclusions and/ or assumptions without knowing the facts. I could not prevent them nor control what they had to say or think. I had control of my thoughts. You see, we will be defeated not by what others say and/ or think about us but by what we say and/or think about ourselves. If God is with us, who can be against us (Romans 8:31)! In all these things we are more than conquerors through Him who loved us (Romans 8:37). We are the head and not the tail (Deut. 28:13). Greater is He that is in us than he who is in the world. I can do all things through Christ who strengthens (Phil. 4:13). It is not just about wishful thinking. It is about faith; declaring it, believing it and acting on it while waiting to win the battle.

One helpful hint while in the battle is to seek more clarity or counsel from the right people. While in the camp, David's brother, Eliab, spoke down on him. David proceeded to seek clarity from others. He knew the importance of reaching out to others. Often times, the first people to talk you out of something is your immediate family members. To realize your full and divine potential, you will have to avoid negative environments at some point in life. Responding to Eliab, David said, "What have I done now? Is there not a cause? Then he turned from him toward another and said the same thing; and these people answered him as the first ones did." 1ˢᵗ Samuel 17:29-30 NKJV. During my wilderness journey, I constantly sought the counsel of my church and prayer family and those who knew and shared in my vision (my church family; The Crossing Church in Livingston, House of Zion Ministry led by Sister Ennette, my sisters Pawla and Emeline and many others (It won't be a good idea to list them to avoid the risk of leaving out some names) who constantly encouraged me to stay in the fight). These folks constantly gave me objective advice which was very helpful in making the right and informed decisions. Even when I felt like giving up, I was told and encouraged not to. Surrounding yourself with the right persons can make a difference between winning and losing. Having people who can see beyond your circumstances or people can see and buy into your vision can make a difference as you are in any fight. Be very open to receiving clarity, counsel and feedback but be thoughtful in following or implementing what you have been told, it is okay to question the motive of the one giving you counsel. I have lived in this world long enough to conclude that some people give you counsel not for your good but for their good or goals. Always seek the clarity and counsel of God through Jesus Christ.

There is a motivational quote that goes, "The road to success is **NOT** straight. There is a curve called Failure, a loop called Confusion, Speed bumps called Friends, red lights called Enemies, caution (yellow) lights called Family. You will have flat tires called Jobs. But if you have a spare wheel (tire) called **Determination**, an Engine called **Perseverance**, an insurance called **Faith**, and a driver called **JESUS**, you will make it to a place called **SUCCESS**."

1) What are some of the invisible battles you are currently fighting?
2) What are some of the battles that you are engaged in that you may consider invincible?
3) Who do you seek clarity from when faced with challenges? Why?
4) Besides God, what are some of your sources for counsel?

5) What is your attitude, belief system and conviction in your battles?

Can you make a listing of some of your battles that may seem unconquerable?

1) _____

2) _____

3) _____

4) _____

5) _____

Can you name 3 to 5 persons or sources that can qualify as your A) Mentor, B) Support C) Coach and D) Counsel

1) _____

2) _____

3) _____

4) _____

5) _____

Prayer

My LORD and my Savior, I commit into Your Mighty hands these unconquerable battles. I know what is impossible to man is very possible to You, LORD. I know You are able and capable of doing the impossible. Omnipotent God, may You exert that mighty power that was exerted when You raised Christ from the dead and seated Him at Your right in the heavenly realms. Thank You LORD for I can do all things through You who strengthens me in Christ Jesus. Amen

Chapter Five

BRINGING THE BREAD OF LIFE TO OTHERS

"Now Jesse said to his son David, "Take this ephah of roasted grain and these ten loaves of bread for your brothers and hurry to their camp.[18] Take along these ten cheeses to the commander of their unit. See how your brothers are and bring back some assurance from them." 1st Samuel 17:17-18 NIV

Your journey to your divine destiny or purpose can start with obeying simple instructions of bringing "bread" to others. When David got up that morning to go about his business of caring for his father's flocks, little did he anticipate going to the war zone to take bread for his siblings and bring back a report about them to his father. But he obeyed when told to do so. It is said "Does the Lord delight in burnt offerings and sacrifices as much as in obeying the Lord? To obey is better than sacrifice, and to heed is better than the fat of rams." 1st Samuel 15:22 NIV. Obeying a father's instructions or directives is paramount to your path to your divine destiny or purpose.

Your journey to your divine purpose also entails leaving your comfort zone into an "uncomfortable zone." Jesse's (David's father) house was his comfort zone. His father's farm where he took care of his animals was his comfort zone. You will agree with me that going to a war zone is not a comfortable place to be. There are lots of risks involved. The mere uncertainty that you may not come back is in itself a huge risk. Many times, you have to get off that couch to get what you want. You have to leave the comfort of your parent's house in order to achieve your full potential. This may even entail going into an unknown territory. Of course David did not know that going to this battle field was going to set off his path to his divine purpose. The point here is not that foreknowledge. Many of us will do things differently if we had the foreknowledge of what lies ahead. But leaving your comfort zone into an unknown world to fulfill your divine purpose is not one of those things we are willing to do.

One interesting thing too is that David did it voluntarily. David was never pressured into taking the bread into the battle field. When his dad asked him, he could have said no. He had that option but he refused to use that nuclear option. There shall come a moment in your life that you should voluntarily take some responsibilities that will change the lives of many. Another point worth mentioning here is that David's brothers did not send an email, text or telephone call to their father to send them food. His father took it upon himself to know that his children will need to be fed, rescued, delivered or whatever the case might be. Mankind too did not ask God to send the "Bread of Life." He did it out of His grace and "according to His riches in glory by Christ Jesus." Philippians 4:19 NKJV. And so our salvation is by grace; "For by grace you have been saved through faith, and that not of yourselves; it is the gift of God, [9] not of works, lest anyone should boast." Ephesians 2:8-9 NKJV. Christ voluntarily laid down His life for you and I.

Obeying your parents is also a Biblical command. In Ephesians 6:1-2 NKJV, the Word of God states "Children, obey your parents in the Lord, for this is right. ² "Honor your father and mother," which is the first commandment with promise." An obedient child brings honor to his parents. Not only so, we are told this is the first commandment with a promise. What is the promise? I am glad you asked. The divine promise which is not limited to a particular person but to everyone who honors his or parents is "that it may be well with you and you may live long on the earth." Ephesians 6:3 NKJV. Maybe this may hold clue to why somethings are not going well in our lives or why some of us do not live long on this planet earth. The act of David obeying his father to bring bread to his brothers, mirrors Christ obeying His Heavenly Father to bring bread to a fallen, hungry and thirsty world. Christ came as the bread of life.

> "And Jesus said to them, "I am the bread of life. He who comes to Me shall never hunger, and he who believes in Me shall never thirst." John 6:35 NKJV He stated that He was not just "the Bread of Life," He was and is "the Living Bread; "I am the living bread which came down from heaven. If anyone eats of this bread, he will live forever; and the bread that I shall give is My flesh, which I shall give for the life of the world." John 6:51 NKJV.

You can safely conclude that when David decided to face the Goliath, he was putting his life on the line for the Israelites. The outcome will ultimately determine not only his fate or life but it determined that of the entire nation. You see, Christ obeyed and honored His father and in the process rescued and redeemed fallen mankind back to God.

One can also safely conclude or deduce that by David willingly taking food to his brothers in the battle field, he was doing good. We are not told that he complained when asked to take food to his brothers. The Bible reminds us to be generous and do good without being tired because in due season, we shall reap the benefits of our generosity and goodness;

> "7 Do not be deceived, God is not mocked; for whatever a man sows, that he will also reap. 8 For he who sows to his flesh will of the flesh reap corruption, but he who sows to the Spirit will of the Spirit reap everlasting life. 9 And let us not grow weary while doing good, for in due season we shall reap if we do not lose heart. 10 Therefore, as we have opportunity, let us do good to all, especially to those who are of the household of faith." Galatians 6:7-10 NKJV.

Before I share some personal stories, let me comment on some few words / phrases from these verses. In verse 9 above, reference is made of Due Season. Our lives are full of seasons (night and day; offseason and on season; up and down; a season of plenty and a season of lack). This also means "in its own time; God's own time (1st Tim 6:15). There shall be moments in our lives when things may not be going the way we want. We shall lack, be in pain, be sick, be unemployed, lose a loved one, be incarcerated just to name these few but we should not give up fellowshipping with the body of Christ, serving others, trusting God, serving in the House of the LORD.

Verse 10 says "as we have the opportunity..." This is a clear indication that the opportunity will not be available at all times. We have little or no control as to when such opportunity shows up. However, we have control over what to do when that opportunity presents itself. There are people God has placed in our lives right now for us to be a blessing to. So the time to be a blessing to fellow brethren is NOW not next time. We have now and we may never have next time or tomorrow. Do not procrastinate as that only inhibits the flow of the grace of the LORD. Whether or not you assist that person NOW will not stop him or her from getting to his or her divine destiny. But how sad it will be when that person shares his or her success story without you being mentioned. So make use of that opportunity NOW while it is still there and do good.

Let me share with you three stories that turned out to be life changing from a simple gesture of doing good when the opportunity presented itself. While in College in my native country of Cameroon, I had gone for about two weeks with no food. One afternoon, we stood in front of a classroom waiting for the opportunity to go into class to secure a seat. You needed to be around the classroom about 2 hours or more in order to secure a seat in class. When the time of class was fast approaching, it became very clear to me that I will not go to class because I was so hungry. I shared this with classmates and told them that I will not attend the class as a result. A classmate took out his wallet and all he can find in it was 10 frs. CFA (a little less than 2 US cents). He handed it to me stating, "I don't know how this will help but I hope it does. I want you to attend the class." I took this money bought some "sugared peanuts (17 of them: yes,

I counted it). I gave this guy 7 of them while hoping to eat 10. He refused to take the 7 peanuts stating that I needed them most. I ate these peanuts and drank some water. I got some energy and was able to go to class. In class the Professor (American Drama class) covered some topics. Three weeks or so later, we had an exam. We were given 9 essay questions from which to choose 6 questions and respond to. Thank God I went to class that day. The 6 questions I chose were covered in class on that day. When the results were out, I was one of few who passed this exam out of the many hundreds of students who took the exam. My classmate and I became very dear friends. You will need so many volumes of books if you wanted to write about our friendship. A little over 3 years after this good gesture of my friend, I had the opportunity to travel to the US. He filled out a form for the Diversity Visa lottery and told me to mail it in when I arrive the US. This I did with the help of another friend and yes, you guess it right. He won. He came here and after some years, he supplied drinking water to his boyhood community and has donated great sums of money to social programs like scholarships, building schools, health programs etc. in our entire community.

A close friend of mine, Lemhan, walked into a public library one day and noticed a guy who was intensely studying. My friend who had recently passed board exams walked up to this guy and inquired of him what and why he was studying. When he learnt that this guy was studying for his board exams but not using the current resources, my friend offered to give him all his resources (Books and CDs). This guy asked Lemhan, how much he was selling these things for but Lemhan, responded he was giving it to him for free. This guy was in disbelief and fully comprehended Lemhan's generosity when J Lemhan actually gave him the books. These two strangers became friends to this date and today more than half of Lemhan's regular customers are as a result of his friend.

While in the "University of ICE", I was helping fellow detainees with their legal documents without charging any fees like most other "jail lawyers" will do. Many of those I helped were released but I could not help myself get out. Many laughed at me questioning why I was able to help others but I could not help myself. After many months of helping others, I got so weary and decided I will no longer help anyone. I "pretended" that I wanted to focus on studying the Bible. I was presented with so many opportunities to help but would not. I was later transferred from NJ to LA and later to AL. I still refused to help but one day my "Christian brothers" confronted me with this "non-helping' attitude. Let it be known that I will help out in other areas and part of my reason for not helping was that others wanted me to charge a "fee' something I was not willing or comfortable to do. Part of my unwillingness to help was also because I can tell of the outcome of those filings and also, I knew what detainees had to go through to make those payments. Anyway, when my brethren "confronted" me telling me it was wrong on my part to refuse to help, and that it was unchristian-like, I began helping again. Few days after I decided to start helping others, a brother in the faith brought his papers for me to help him. In going through his papers, I found a paper in it which will become the breakthrough I have been looking and praying for. Thanks to God and to that paper, I was later released from "university of ICE."

1) What is it that your heavenly father has asked you to do?
2) How are you honoring your earthly parents?

3) What opportunities has God presented you with to help a fellow human being?

4) How are you making a difference in someone's life?

Can you list 3 to 5 persons who can testify that you have made a difference in their lives or who can say they won't be where they today are if not of you?

1) _____

2) _____

3) _____

4) _____

5) _____

Prayer

Lord, Jesus. You are the Bread of Life that nourishes and supports my Spiritual life. You are the Bread that came down from heaven. Feed me with this Bread that I may never hunger again. May I know that I cannot live by bread alone but by every Word that comes out of your Mouth. May I never desire any food but Christ. Grant me Your grace, faith and the spirit of Obedience that I may abide in You in Christ Jesus. Amen

Chapter Six

RESOURCES AND/ OR SKILLS IN FACING YOUR GOLIATHS: "OBEDIENCE IS BETTER THAN SACRIFICE."

"So David rose early in the morning, left the sheep with a keeper, and took *the things* and went as Jesse had commanded him. And he came to the camp as the army was going out to the fight and shouting for the battle. [21] For Israel and the Philistines had drawn up in battle array, army against army" 1st Samuel 17:20 NKJV

In order to face your goliaths, you will need to have certain spirits and certain resources to successfully face these goliaths. These resources may not be exactly the same in your situation as each situation may call for different skills and/ or resources. But let's examine what David used in order to successfully go into battle field to face his goliath. First he had the spirit of Obedience (to the LORD), then the spirit to arise and act in the morning and finally the spirit to delegate certain or current responsibilities.

David was an obedient child hence and easily obeyed his father's instructions. As I pointed in the previous chapter, David, when told by his father to bring bread to his brothers in the battlefield and to bring back words about them, obediently agreed to do as asked. He did not complain, whine or ask many questions as to why him. Why was David chosen to go to the battle field and not the others? In 1st Samuel 16:10-11, the Bible clearly implies that Jesse, David's father had 8 sons of which David was the youngest. In 1st Chronicles 2:13-15, it names Jesse's 7 children of whom David was the youngest. In 1st Samuel 17:13, we are told 3 of Jesse's sons were in the battlefield.

> "The three oldest sons of Jesse had gone to follow Saul to the battle. The names of his three sons who went to the battle were Eliab the firstborn, next to him Abinadab, and the third Shammah. ¹⁴ David *was* the youngest. And the three oldest followed Saul. ¹⁵ But David occasionally went and returned from Saul to feed his father's sheep at Bethlehem" 1st Samuel 17:13-15 NKJV

So where were the other children or sons? Why did Jesse not send them? Could this give credence to the fact that David was an obedient child?

Some of the battles we face originate in the spiritual realm and requires us to battle these challenges in spirit. This requires us to be obedient to the LORD else we will not be able to successfully face these battles. In Joshua 5:6, we are told that the Israelites moved around in the wilderness and many of military age died because they were not obedient to God, "The Israelites had moved about in the wilderness forty years until all the men who were of military age when they left Egypt had died, since they had not obeyed the LORD. For the LORD had sworn to them that they would not see the land he had solemnly promised their ancestors to give us, a land flowing with milk and honey." In Luke 11:28 NIV, Jesus is quoted as saying "…Blessed rather are those who hear the word of God and obey it." The battle is technically not us but it is God's (2nd Chronicles 20:15) hence our obedience is necessary. And since most of our battles are spiritual, we do not need physical weapons to battle them with. In 2nd Corinthians 10:4-6 NKJV the Bible states "For the weapons of our warfare *are* not carnal but mighty in God for pulling down strongholds, casting down arguments and every high thing that exalts itself against the knowledge of God, bringing every thought into captivity to the obedience of Christ, and being ready to punish all disobedience when your obedience is fulfilled." If we live in obedience of the Word of God, we will easily overcome every goliath that comes our way and He promises us that if we obey Him, we will be His treasured possession. "Now if you obey me fully and keep my covenant, then out of all nations you will be my treasured possession. Although the whole earth is mine," Exodus 19:5 NIV

The Bible is full of instances where it required the absolute obedience of God for His children to overcome the goliaths they were facing at the time. When Joshua and the children of Israel were to enter Jericho, the LORD instructed them as follows "You shall march around the city, all you men of war; you shall go all around the city once. This you shall do six days. ⁴ And seven priests shall bear seven trumpets of rams' horns before the ark. But the seventh day you shall march around the city seven times, and the priests shall blow the trumpets. ⁵ It shall come to pass, when they make a long *blast* with the ram's horn, *and* when you hear the sound of the trumpet, that all the people shall shout with a great shout; then the wall of the city will fall down flat. And the people shall go up every man straight before him." Joshua 6:3-5 NKJV. The LORD instructed Gideon to burnt down the altars in his father's house (Judges 6:25) and to reduce his army to 300 men to fight the Midianites (Judges 7). Samson was called to a life of obedience "Now therefore, please be careful not to drink wine or similar drink, and not to eat anything unclean. For behold, you shall conceive and bear a son. And no razor shall come upon his head, for the child shall be a *Nazirite to God from the womb; and he shall begin to deliver Israel out of the hand of the Philistines*" (Judges 13:4-5 NKJV). You can find the entire story of Samson in Judges chapters 13 through 16 where you can also see how disobedience caused his life. Jesus lived a life of obedience. In Psalm 119:2 NIV we are told, "Blessed are they who keep His statutes and seek Him with all their heart." When I read the Bible, it is clear that the LORD's world was designed to be the first two chapters of the Bible (Genesis 1 and 2). After creation, God placed man in the garden for man to "tend and keep it" and He gave man an instruction not to eat of the tree of the knowledge of good and evil.

> "Then the LORD GOD TOOK THE MAN AND PUT HIM IN THE GARDEN OF EDEN TO TEND AND KEEP IT. [16] And the LORD GOD COMMANDED THE MAN, SAYING, "OF EVERY TREE OF THE GARDEN YOU MAY FREELY EAT; [17] but of the tree of the knowledge of good and evil you shall not eat, for in the day that you eat of it you shall surely die." Genesis 2:15-17 NKJV

This was a simple instruction for man to obey but when Genesis

3 opens up, we are presented with man eating the fruit from the tree of knowledge of good and evil. Man did not sin nor fall by the mere fact of eating the fruit. But his fall was a disobedience to God's instructions. From this moment on, the rest of the Bible was written outlining God's continued effort to rescue humanity from our disobedience and to draw man closer to Himself.

How you start your day makes a difference as to how the rest of the day will proceed. David set out about the day's activities by first acting early in the morning. The night represents darkness and the enemy operates in the dark. Darkness or night represents death. The morning represents light. Light is Christ and it is in the light or day (morning) that our savior operates. "I must work the works of Him who sent Me while it is day; *the* night is coming when no one can work." John 9:4 NKJV

As believers, we are called to work during the day when there is light. Elkanah and his wife, Hannah, set out to go worship the LORD in Shiloh. 1st Samuel 1:19. It is in the morning that Abraham arose and left with Isaac to offer him as a sacrifice Genesis 22:3. It is in the morning that Joshua and the Israelites arose and went to the bank of River Jordan ready to cross over Joshua 3:1. The LORD told Moses to go before Pharaoh in the morning (Exodus 7:15; 8:20; 9:13; 34:2-4). It is in the morning that Jacob arose and built a memorial at Bethel after his dream Genesis 28:18. The Bible is full of activities that take place in the morning (Genesis 19:27-28; Ezekiel 12:8; Ezekiel 46:13-15 just to name these few). You are encouraged to set your daily plans first thing in the morning. You should set your weekly goals on the first day of the week. All monthly goals should be set in the first day of the month and all annual goals should be set in the first month of the year. I also challenge and encourage you to start your days on the knees. What a joy it is to start off your day in the presence of the LORD. Start the day on your knees with a prayer. Start by reading and meditating on a verse or some verses.

One other thing about morning is that we must learn to act or decide early on in opportunities that present itself. You do not need to spend countless time thinking or contemplating on whether or not you should capitalize on such opportunities. Early decisions and actions will always lead to great success. Do not get me wrong. I am not advocating that you take very risky ill informed decisions or actions but if you know it is the Will of God, decide and act on it immediately. Spending countless hours pondering on it only opens up the doors for the enemy to destroy your plans. When I met my wife and knew that she was the woman God has destined for me, I immediately proposed to her and we were married shortly after. I did not have to wait too long. I knew that was the person God had chosen for me and so there was no need waiting unnecessarily. Some have questioned that decision but I believe it is the Will of God and I am trusting Him to lead, guide and control the marriage. Not only do you have to arise in the morning to face your goliaths, you have to delegate certain of your responsibilities.

In line with acting in the morning is also the concept of time or timing. Time and perfect timing is of great importance in our daily living. David left the house in the morning and arrived the battle just in time for the enemy (Goliath) to step up and challenge the Israelites. Just imagine for a minute that David overslept or David left the house way too early; he probably could have missed the opportunity to see and hear Goliath. Many believers today struggle with time management while some find themselves "over sleeping" while life and business is going on. And by the way, when "the

53

champion, the Philistine of Gath, Goliath by name" came up and spoke those words defying Israel and "David heard them," did any of the Israelites hear them? Or they simply ran as they saw him? It is very interesting that the Bible clearly names David to have heard these words without naming others. Could it be that the hearing of these words took on a deeper meaning when it came to David? Look at the parables of the 4 soils presented in Matthew 13:1-23; Mark 4:1-20 and Luke 8:1-15. The soils al receive the same seed from the same sower but each produces different outcomes. We are all hear or will hear the Word of God but not all will respond to it by receiving the Word as the Truth. May you never be one of those to reject the Word of God.

Another requirement for us to successfully engage in our battles is to delegate some of our current duties. Many times, the battles we engage in can be so intense that it will require our complete focus and hence the necessity to delegate some of our jobs descriptions. David understood he could not take the sheep with him to the battlefield. He entrusted that responsibility to a keeper ("So David rose early in the morning, left the sheep with a keeper" verse 20). Delegating things does not necessarily mean that you have given away your responsibility. It also does not mean that you are a lazy person or that you do not know how to carry out the responsibility. If you are hiding your lack of know how or your laziness behind delegating, then you have failed. The goal of delegating should be to reduce the work load on your shoulder while giving others the opportunity to excel in such areas. This in effect leads to divesting and replicating leadership. Let's take for instance the case of Moses where Moses' father in law advises Moses to select God fearing men and delegate some of his duties to them.

"And so it was, on the next day, that Moses sat to judge the people; and the people stood before Moses from morning until evening. ¹⁴ So when Moses' father-in-law saw all that he did for the people, he said, "What *is* this thing that you are doing for the people? Why do you alone [f]sit, and all the people stand before you from morning until evening?"

¹⁵ And Moses said to his father-in-law, "Because the people come to me to inquire of God. ¹⁶ When they have a [g]difficulty, they come to me, and I judge between one and another; and I make known the statutes of God and His laws."

¹⁷ So Moses' father-in-law said to him, "The thing that you do *is* not good. ¹⁸ Both you and these people who *are* with you will surely wear yourselves out. For this thing *is* too much for you; you are not able to perform it by yourself. ¹⁹ Listen now to my voice; I will give you [h]counsel, and God will be with you: Stand before God for the people, so that you may bring the difficulties to God. ²⁰ And you shall teach them the statutes and the laws, and show them the way in which they must walk and the work they must do. ²¹ Moreover you shall select from all the people able men, such as fear God, men of truth, hating covetousness; and place *such* over them *to be* rulers of thousands, rulers of hundreds, rulers of fifties, and rulers of tens. ²² And let them judge the people at all times. Then it will be *that* every great matter they shall bring to you, but every small matter they

themselves shall judge. So it will be easier for you, for they will bear *the burden* with you. ²³ If you do this thing, and God *so* commands you, then you will be able to endure, and all this people will also go to their place in peace." Exodus 18:13-23 NKJV

Let us look at another instance where duties were delegated (division of labor). In Exodus 17, when the Amalekites came against the Israelites, Moses went to intercede before God for Israel while he delegated the duties of leading the Israelites in the battle to Joshua.

"Now Amalek came and fought with Israel in Rephidim. ⁹ And Moses said to Joshua, "Choose us some men and go out, fight with Amalek. Tomorrow I will stand on the top of the hill with the rod of God in my hand." ¹⁰ So Joshua did as Moses said to him, and fought with Amalek. And Moses, Aaron, and Hur went up to the top of the hill. ¹¹ And so it was, when Moses held up his hand, that Israel prevailed; and when he let down his hand, Amalek prevailed. ¹² But Moses' hands *became*[e]heavy; so they took a stone and put *it* under him, and he sat on it. And Aaron and Hur supported his hands, one on one side, and the other on the other side; and his hands were steady until the going down of the sun. ¹³ So Joshua defeated Amalek and his people with the edge of the sword." Ex. 17:8-13 NKJV

Delegating to others is not a sign of weakness unless you are delegating because you do not know what to do and are lazy to learn or because you cannot properly manage your time. The ability to delegate is actually an asset for as long as you are delegating for good reasons.

1) Are you being obedient to the word of God?
2) In what areas of your life are you exhibiting disobedience?
3) What responsibilities are you about to engage in or are you currently engaged in?
4) What are some of the responsibilities that you can delegate to others (siblings, children, co-workers, spouse etc.) and why have you not delegated these responsibilities before now or why do you not want to delegate these responsibilities?
5) What is your Time Management skill like?

Can you list 3 to 5 times you have accomplished or missed because you either arrive on time or too early / too late?

1) _____
2) _____
3) _____
4) _____
5) _____

Prayer

Oh LORD, grant me the grace and wisdom to be able to delegate some of the many tasks that are keeping me from achieving my full divine purpose. I pray that I will be obedient to You just as You were so obedient to death. Help me Oh LORD to take away any obstacle that might stand in the way of me being obedient to You. As you so loved the world that You gave Your only begotten child, help us to love You. May I not be conformed to this world even though I live in it. May I surrender my thoughts, words and actions to Will and Control this day for Christ Sake. Amen

Chapter Seven

YOUR BATTLEFIELD IS WHERE
YOUR CHANGE FIRST OCCURS

"Now the Israelites had been saying, "Do you see how this man keeps coming out? He comes out to defy Israel. The king will give great wealth to the man who kills him. He will also give him his daughter in marriage and will exempt his family from taxes in Israel." 1ˢᵗ Samuel 17:25 NIV

We often think that change in our circumstance occurs at the end of our battles. That is not the case in some instances. Change actually begins in our battles. When David was told of some of the benefits that will accrue to the one (and his family) who kills goliath, he began to immediately notice some change within. He experienced a mental change which urged him to make sure what he heard was correct. "Then David spoke to the men who stood by him, saying, "What shall be done for the man who kills this Philistine and takes away the reproach from Israel?" 1ˢᵗ Samuel 17:26 NKJV. One ready for change should always ask probing questions to gain a better understanding. Do not get caught up in asking so many questions without having the gained knowledge change your mindset or view. Always maintain an open mind and when you come across something new, let it poke your curiosity. You also have to be attentive and have good listening skills. It is very possible that in a battlefield, things are very noisy and crazy that requires an extra attentiveness. It is also possible that in a "military expedition" as this, things are discussed silently so as not to give away military secrets and strategies. In either scenario, you have to bring your A game in listening and paying attention to details.

Another thing worth noting here is that when there is a calling or anointing on your life, be ready to face some battles in your life. David's presence in the battlefield comes shortly after the Prophet Samuel had anointed him as the future king…"So he sent for him and had him brought in. He was glowing with health and had a fine appearance and handsome features. Then the LORD said, "Rise and anoint him; this is the one." 1ˢᵗ Samuel 16:12 NIV. Samuel had just anointed David the future king. You will think that he should be taken straight to the palace or he should live a trouble free life. But that is not how it operates in God's kingdom. When God calls or anoints you, it takes some time before the thing actually materializes in the physical realm. Let's point to some few cases in the Bible. God first appeared to Abraham (called Abram at the time) and made promises to him when he was 75 years old in Genesis 12. "Now the LORD had said to Abram: Get out of your country, from your family and from your father's house, to a land that I will show you. ²I will make you a great nation; I will bless you and make your name great; And you shall be a blessing. ³I will bless those who bless you, And I will curse him who curses you; And in you all the families of the earth shall be blessed." Genesis 12:1-3 NKJV. God reminds Abraham of this promise again in Genesis 17 when Abraham is now 99 years old. "When Abram was ninety-nine years old, the LORD APPEARED TO ABRAM AND SAID TO HIM, "I *am* [a]Almighty God; walk before Me and be blameless. ²And I will make My covenant between Me and you, and will multiply you exceedingly." ³Then Abram fell on his face, and God talked with him, saying: ⁴"As for Me, behold, My covenant is with you, and you shall be a father of [b]many nations. ⁵ No longer shall your name be called [c]Abram, but your name shall be [d]Abraham; for I have made you a father of [e]many nations. ⁶I will make you exceedingly fruitful; and I will make nations of you, and kings shall come from you. ⁷And I will establish My covenant between Me and you and your descendants after you in their generations, for an everlasting covenant, to be God to you and your descendants after you. ⁸Also I give to you and your descendants after you the land in[f] which you are a stranger, all the land of Canaan, as an everlasting possession; and I will be their God." Genesis 17:1-8 NKJV. A few things I should quickly point out here. This is where God changes Abraham's name from Abram to Abraham. His promise now is that Abraham will be a father of nations not just a great nation as was the case in Genesis 12. Now let us take the case of Joseph. He was just 17 when he first had his dreams (Genesis 37). His brothers will later sell him into slavery to the Medianites who in turn sold him to Potiphar (Genesis 37:12-36). Joseph will later be thrown into jail (Genesis 39) and it is not until Joseph is 30 that his dreams actually materializes in the physical realm (Genesis 41: 41; reference Genesis chapters 37 to 47 for Joseph's story).

In my early years, my grandfather, told me on many occasions that I will follow his footsteps but I was not ready to hear this. I looked at his financial situation as a Senior Pastor (he oversaw so many churches) and I was not ready to accept such a state. I did not see anything appealing with becoming a voice for the kingdom. I always envisioned myself becoming a governor, a diplomat, an international lawyer and why not the president of the country. I knew I had what it takes to become any of these professionals. However, my grandfather, a Man of God (with his unique story of how he became a MOG), saw something in me that no one else in the family saw. With all the respect and love I had for my granny, this was one area I was going to disobey him and I will go on to do all it takes to stay clear from nursing any thoughts of getting into ministry. At some point in life, I seriously began nursing the idea of getting more involved in ministry with the hope of living out my granny's wish. Many in the faith encouraged and counseled me on pursuing this "calling." I quickly dismissed any encouragements and counsel stating that going into ministry was only a matter of trying to please my granny and not me or God. But truth is that I was disobedient not only to my granny but also to God. In the year of my greatest trial, I had three visions and a clear "encounter" with the LORD in which He asked me 5 questions to make clear my relationship with Him. The 5th question ("While on earth, did you serve me as you were supposed to serve me?") got me thinking. Shortly after these visions, I was led off to "University of ICE". It is in "University of ICE" that I will begin to witness a transformation in my mind or thinking. I had time to reflect on these issues and I began to earnestly seek the LORD. When I began to earnestly seek Him, He made Himself available as promised in Jeremiah 29:13-14 NKJV "And you will seek Me and find Me, when you search for Me with all your heart. I will be found by you, says the Lord, and I will bring you back from your captivity; I will gather you from all the nations and from all the places where I have driven you, says the Lord, and I will bring you to the place from which I cause you to be carried away captive." Also reference 1st Chronicles 28:9, 2nd Chronicles 15:2. During my stay (or training as I often call it) in the "University of ICE," I had countless encounters with the LORD that have forever shaped my thinking, my future and my life.

While in the battle, do not look at your circumstance; look at your God. Let your circumstance not define you or your relationship with God. Looking at your circumstance breaths fear but looking at God breathes faith.

1) What are some of the challenges that you are faced with right now that can be attributed to you becoming a Christian (a follower of Christ)?
2) Briefly describe some of the mental changes or transformations since you became a believer in and a follower of Christ?
3) What are some of your most recent challenges or battles?
4) Briefly describe some of your mental transformations that took place during or after these most recent challenge or challenges listed in item 3 above?

List 3 to 5 probing questions you used during your most recent challenge that helped you gained a better understanding of the situation.

1) _____
2) _____
3) _____
4) _____
5) _____

Prayer

My Lord and my Savior, You are my refuge and my strength. You are my ever present help in times of troubles. Grant me the grace to believe these Words. I pray Oh LORD that my current circumstance will not dictate or define my relationship with You. I pray Oh LORD, that I will keep my eyes focus on You at all times for Christ sake. Thank You LORD for being present in my boat (challenge). Your presence is all that I need in Jesus Mighty Name. Amen

Chapter Eight

DON'T LET YOUR FAMILY AND/ OR YOUR PAST HOLD YOU BACK

"Never let the past spoil your present or govern your future." – Author Unknown

An unknown author was remarked "the road to success is NOT straight. There is a curve called Failure, a loop called Confusion, Speed bumps called Friends, red lights called Enemies, caution (Yellow) lights called Family. You will have flat tires called Jobs. But if you have a spare wheel (tire) called Determination, an Engine called Perseverance, an Insurance called Faith, and a driver called JESUS, you will make it to a place called SUCCESS." This statement is not far from the truth. Many of us will agree with me that we have tried to embark on certain ventures but only to be advised against our dreams by friends and family. This concept is not new as it has some of its roots dating back to David's days.

"When Eliab, David's oldest brother, heard him speaking with the men, he burned with anger at him and asked, "Why have you come down here? And with whom did you leave those few sheep in the wilderness? I know how conceited you are and how wicked your heart is; you came down only to watch the battle."

"Now what have I done?" said David. "Can't I even speak?" 1st Samuel 17:28-29 NIV

Notice here that Eliab, David's elder brother does not only question him for coming down but he does so with great anger. Our friends and family will always find ways to talk us out of our dreams and they will go as far as calling us names. I sat down and painfully listened to a story by Zuberi who was so gifted in soccer (also academically gifted) but never exploited those soccer gifts because of his family's influence. Zuberi was so good or gifted in soccer that the school elected him to captain the team while still in his junior years. Captainship was reserved for the senior and more adult students. Captainship was not so much based on leadership skills but on how gifted you were with the game. Despite his gifts, the family did everything to destroy his soccer ambition preventing him from going to soccer practice. Some of the guys who played with Zuberi and looked up to him will go on to play in elite clubs while one or two represented the country at the national level. As Zuberi shared his stories and his collection of pictures of his playing days, you could see him visibly upset and you can hear a tone of disappointment in his voice. This notion of a family destroying the dreams of a person is so rampant within the African community especially if such a dream conflicts with "formal or general" education. An African parent will do all it takes to re-direct a child's passion or giftedness to "formal or general" education. Do not get me wrong, as an educator, I am a big fan of "formal" education but to push "formal" education at the total sacrifice of other areas of life is damaging. I recently met a couple whose son, Lekan, was just starting off in his second year at a prestigious University on a $60000 scholarship. He was majoring in Economics and Finance. During Lekan's first year of studies, he developed an application that can greatly increase your success rate at investing in stocks. He used this application to generate over $48,000 while working on a part time basis. Some well-known investors made an offer to purchase this application for a few million dollars but the young man rejected the offer given the potential he saw in his application. Lekan suggested to his parents that he wanted to leave school so that he can concentrate on his passion or gift but this was a discussion his parents will not even entertain. He even pleaded that they should allow him to enroll in school on a part time basis so he can work on his money making venture on a "full time" schedule but his parents were still not having any of that. Why? They wanted him to concentrate on education ("formal") and get at least a Bachelor's degree before "experimenting" in his gifts or passion. My position was for Lekan to raise enough money that can cover his education for 1 to 2 years and give this money to his parents who will invest it under their custody in low risk products. This may convince them to allow him to enroll in classes on a part time basis while engaging in his venture on a full time. He can the money placed under the custody of his parents in the future to cover any educational expenses should his venture fail.

Not only will friends and family discourage you from pursing your divine purpose by talking you away from it, they will do so by reminding you of your past or your past responsibilities. They will rather see you stuck in your current or past responsibilities. Notice how Eliab confines David to a sheep keeper. While Eliab's question ("And with whom did you leave those few sheep in the wilderness?") is a very legitimate question, the intent behind it makes a difference. He is not asking such a genuine question out of concern but he is doing so negatively and confining David to that role. Recall a similar situation occurred with Jesus too

> "Is this not the carpenter's son? Is not His mother called Mary? And His brothers James, Joses, Simon, and Judas? And His sisters, are they not all with us? Where then did this *Man* get all these things?" So they were offended at Him. But Jesus said to them, "A prophet is not without honor except in his own country and in his own house." Matt 13:55-57 NKJV

Family and friends will even attempt to tell you how well they know you more than you know yourself. Read the words of Eliab again ("I know how conceited you are and how wicked your heart is; you came down only to watch the battle"). Up to this time, nothing in David's past makes us know that he is a conceited fellow, nothing makes us know that he is a wicked fellow. On the contrary, we know David as a responsible young man, who is dedicated to preserving the family wealth, was a gifted and obedient young man (1st Samuel 16:14-23).

When you come to receive, know and serve God, many will always look for ways to remind you of your past. And your past will always come up against you. But let none of these keep you from reaping the full benefits of your new found passion or relationship. Let none of these keep you away from pursing your divine purpose.

Make every effort to live your life for now and the future and not for the past. That past is gone and you have no control over it again. Thank God you "used to be..." but you are no longer where you used to be or who you used to be. As Steve Maraboli once said, ""If people refuse to look at you in a new light and they can only see you for what you were, only see you for the mistakes you've made, if they don't realize that you are not your mistakes, then they have to go." Or "Renew, release, let go. Yesterday's gone. There's nothing you can do to bring it back. You can't "should've" done something. You can only DO something. Renew yourself. Release that attachment. Today is a new day!" And as L. Ron Hubbard stated, "Never regret yesterday. Life is in you today, and you make your tomorrow." Nelson Mandela in putting behind his past once remarked "As I walked out the door toward the gate that would lead to freedom, I knew that if I did not leave all the anger, hatred and bitterness behind, that I would still be in prison."

The Bible is so clear about cautioning us against looking back or in effect considering giving much value to our past. Recall the stories when God was about to destroy Sodom and Gomorrah in Genesis 19. Lot and the family were told to get out of town without looking back (verse 19), "So it came to pass, when they had brought them outside, that he said, escape for your life, do not look behind you nor stay anywhere in the plain...But his wife looked back behind him and she became a pillar of salt." Paul in writing to the church in Philippi states, "Brethren, I do not count myself to have apprehended; but one thing I do, forgetting those things which are behind and reaching forward to those things which are ahead, [14] I press toward the goal for the prize of the upward call of God in Christ Jesus" Philippians 3:13 NKJV. Also, in Paul's letter to the church in Corinth, we are reminded that, "if anyone is in Christ, the new creation has come; the old has gone, the new is here" 2ⁿᵈ Corinthians 5:17 NIV. Jesus Himself encourages us when he states "No one who puts his hand to the plow and looks back is fit for the kingdom of God." Luke 9:62 RSV.

I was a history student and I still love history but I do not allow history to control or dictate my now and my tomorrow. If one depended on history, you will not be reading these words penned by me today. If you had asked some of my friends some years ago that I will be today singing the praises of the Living God, they will bet their lives on it. Why? Because at some point in my late teenage years and early 20s, I was living in the world. During these years, I walked away from the "calling." I found most of my pleasure in the things of the world. Some today will want to hold me to that past. Some will want to remind me of that past. But I chose not to be held hostage to that past. It is gone, it is history, it cannot hold me captive. I can only learn from it and not live in it.

1) What are some of the areas of your life in which your family and friends are preventing you from meeting your God given potential

2) What areas of your life is your past holding you back?

3) How were you able or how are you able to overcome these goliaths that stand in your way in the name of family, friends or your pasts

List 3 to 5 areas in which you think your family or your past is holding you back from fulfilling your divine purpose?

1) _____

2) _____

3) _____

4) _____

5) _____

Prayer

Merciful and faithful God, I pray the Blood of Jesus will help off root those things in the past that is hindering Your child from fulfilling that which he or she was destined for. I pray Your child will let go the past and focus on the God of NOW, the God who has a plan to give us hope and a future and not a past. May _____ (your name) not be held captive to his or her past in Jesus Mighty Name. Amen

Chapter Nine

BELIEVE IN YOURSELF AND IN YOUR GOD

When you get into a battle, the first step to success is to believe in yourself and your God. As a matter of fact, I will strongly suggest that if you do not believe in yourself and if you have no confidence in yourself, do not even waste your time getting into the fight. As you have learnt in the previous chapter, family, friends and others will always want to talk you out of your ventures so relying on them is already the first assurance of failure. Let us take a close look at how the goliath reacted when he saw David.

> *"He looked David over and saw that he was little more than a boy, glowing with health and handsome, and he despised him. He said to David, "Am I a dog, that you come at me with sticks?" And the Philistine cursed David by his gods. "Come here," he said, "and I'll give your flesh to the birds and the wild animals!" 1 Samuel 17:42-44 NIV*

Goliath despised him. Other versions say "disdained him." Those (despise and disdain) are very strong words. Battles are psychological or mental in nature. So if you can psychologically or mentally beat your opponent, your chances of winning the actual fight is high. While this is or may be expected from one's opponents, let's take a look at what Saul said to David when David decided he was going to go up against goliath:

> *"You are not able to go out against this Philistine and fight him; you are only a young man, and he has been a warrior from his youth." 1 Samuel 17:33 NIV*

How discouraging this could be coming from the leader of the people. How sad? Some leaders have talked their subordinates out of bringing their full potential on the table. Parents have talked their children out of living out their full potential. Just because one has not been doing something in the past or from his youth does not preclude him or her from knowing how to do it. Just because one is still a "young man" does not preclude one from having the best idea that can solve that major problem that is keeping people up at night. This reminds me of the story where Jesus feeds 5000 men plus women and children with 5 loaves of bread and 2 fishes (John 6:1-14). Where did the bread and fish come from? It came from a little boy (John 6:9). As leaders, elders or people of position / influence, let us not discount others and their ideas just because of who they are. Major companies like Microsoft, Facebook, Google, Apple etc. that have revolutionized today's world were founded by youngsters not with any high degree of academic credentials next to their names.

When in a battle, besides believing in yourself or having confidence in yourself, you must know yourself. I like the response David gave Saul. It is clear that David knew who he was. He was a fighter, a conqueror, and a victor. He knew some of the things he has accomplished in the past. Above all, he knew he was and is one who trusted in the LORD.

> "But David said to Saul, "Your servant used to keep his father's sheep, and when a lion or a bear came and took a lamb out of the flock, [35] I went out after it and struck it, and delivered *the lamb* from its mouth; and when it arose against me, I caught *it* by its beard, and struck and killed it. [36] Your servant has killed both lion and bear; and this uncircumcised Philistine will be like one of them, seeing he has defied the armies of the living God." [37] Moreover David said, "The LORD, WHO DELIVERED ME FROM THE PAW OF THE LION AND FROM THE PAW OF THE BEAR, HE WILL DELIVER ME FROM THE HAND OF THIS PHILISTINE." 1 SAMUEL 17: 34-37 NKJV

This is one instance I will recommend your past should come into play. David had to look into his past accomplishments and successes ("Your servant used to keep his father's sheep, and when a lion or a bear came and took a lamb out of the flock, I went out after it and struck it, and delivered the lamb from its mouth; and when it arose against me, I caught it by its beard, and struck and killed it. Your servant has killed both lion and bear...") to encourage himself and face current challenges. And David knew who (God) delivered him in the past and if He did it then, He will do it again. Why? He is the same God. He never changes. If He did yesterday, He will do it again. Our circumstances may change but our God does not. David also knows that "No one who hopes in you will ever be put to shame, but shame will come on those who are treacherous without cause" Psalm 25:3. Many of us when faced with challenges forget who we are and forget what we have with us or who is in us. "You are of God, little children, and have overcome them, because He who is in you is greater than he who is in the world." 1st John 4:4 NKJV

I cannot over emphasize the point how important it is for you to believe in you. Very few, if at all there will be any, will believe in you. When the Prophet, Samuel, was sent to anoint one of Jesse's sons as the future king of Israel, David presented all his children without David. It is not until the prophet asked of other children that he was told that David was out in the fields mending the flocks.

> *"Thus Jesse made seven of his sons pass before Samuel. And Samuel said to Jesse, "The LORD HAS NOT CHOSEN THESE." ¹¹ And Samuel said to Jesse, "Are all the young men here?" Then he said, "There remains yet the youngest, and there he is, keeping the sheep." And Samuel said to Jesse, "Send and bring him. For we will not sit down till he comes here." So he sent and brought him in. Now he was ruddy, with ʃbright eyes, and good-looking. And the LORD SAID, "ARISE, ANOINT HIM; FOR THIS is the one!" 1st Samuel 16:10-12 NKJV*

We can safely deduce that even Samuel himself, the Man of God, did not believe in David. Recall that when Eliab came before Samuel, he concluded that Eliab must be the one the LORD had chosen given his physical built. But the LORD informed him that He is not interested in one's outward appearance but rather He is interested in one's inward appearance.

> "So it was, when they came, that he looked at Eliab and said, "Surely the LORD'S ANOINTED IS before Him!" But the LORD SAID TO SAMUEL, "DO NOT LOOK AT HIS APPEARANCE OR AT HIS PHYSICAL STATURE, BECAUSE I HAVE [c]refused him. For the LORD DOES not see as man sees; for man looks at the outward appearance, but the LORD LOOKS AT THE HEART." 1st Samuel 16:6-7 NKJV

Your appearance and other inherent shortcomings or flaws in you will not hold you back from your divine appointment or purpose. What stands in the way of your future is only you, your belief and your God. I have come across many who will blame all their failures on others but themselves. They will blame their failures on what they do not have forgetting to realize that they have all that it takes to fight their battles. Take the classic case of blind Bartemaeus (Mark 10:46-52). While he sat by the road begging, he heard that Jesus was passing by and "he began to cry out and say Jesus, Son of David, have mercy on me!" (the use of his mouth). Despite the fact that he did not have sight, he knew he had ears to hear and a mouth to speak and he made good use of these things he had. You must be your greatest advocate besides God. You must take full ownership, control and responsibility of your state of being and your future. No one should dictate your state of being. No one should own your life. Whatever future you want for yourself, you can build it. No one will do it for you and it is not in the interest of anyone to see you change your current state of being.

Others have everything to gain to see you maintain your current status quo. The only one you should surrender to is your God. He is the only one that finds joy in your success, prosperity, peace and comfort. He is the only one that is interested in your success and He is "able to do exceedingly abundantly above all that we ask or think, according to the power that works in us" and He will do it.

1) Who are those in your life that are constantly reminding you that you cannot accomplish XYZ?
2) What are some of the excuses you have been telling yourself that you cannot go to school, start a business, get married, become financially independent, do the will of God, pursue / accomplish your divine purpose etc.?
3) In what or whom do you put your trust in?
4) Share some of your experiences in which your former boss or leader tried to discourage you from an action?

Can you list 3 to 5 areas in which you are doubting yourself

1) _____
2) _____
3) _____
4) _____
5) _____

List 3 to 5 things in which you whole heartedly trusted God and yourself and it turned out as desired?

1) _____
2) _____

3) _____

4) _____

5) _____

Prayer

Faithful and holy Father, help me LORD, to put my trust in You for those who put their trust in will not be put to shame. I pray O LORD that I will abide in You and Your Word will abide in me. Grant me the grace to mediate on Your Word day and night and that I may be able to do everything in it. May Your presence never depart from me in Jesus Mighty Name. Amen

Chapter Ten

BY HIS SPIRIT ALONE

"So He said to me, "This is the word of the LORD to Zerubbabel: 'Not by might nor by power, but by my Spirit,' says the LORD Almighty."
Zechariah 4:6 NIV

How we fight our battles and how we see those battles will determine the outcome of our battles. Our approach to and perception of our battles can greatly influence the outcome.

"David said to the Philistine, "You come against me with sword and spear and javelin, but I come against you in the name of the Lord Almighty, the God of the armies of Israel, whom you have defied. **46** This day the LORD will deliver you into my hands, and I'll strike you down and cut off your head. This very day I will give the carcasses of the Philistine army to the birds and the wild animals, and the whole world will know that there is a God in Israel. **47** All those gathered here will know that it is not by sword or spear that the Lord saves; for the battle is the Lord's, and he will give all of you into our hands." 1st Samuel 17:45-47 NIV

Our battles are best fought and won not by our military might, not by our talents, beauty, skills, bank accounts but by the Spirit of the Living God. When many of us come against any obstacle or challenges, we are quick to look at our physical or visible gifts. But this should not be the classic case with believers or Christians. When the Israelites came before the Philistines, they were terrified by goliath's physical or visible attributes and the words that came out of his mouth.

"And a champion went out from the camp of the Philistines, named Goliath, from Gath, whose height *was* six cubits and a span. ⁵ *He had* a bronze helmet on his head, and he *was* [a]armed with a coat of mail, and the weight of the coat *was* five thousand shekels of bronze. ⁶ And *he had* bronze armor on his legs and a bronze javelin between his shoulders. ⁷ Now the staff of his spear *was* like a weaver's beam, and his iron spearhead *weighed* six hundred shekels; and a shield-bearer went before him. ⁸ Then he stood and cried out to the armies of Israel, and said to them, "Why have you come out to line up for battle? *Am* I not a Philistine, and you the servants of Saul? Choose a man for yourselves, and let him come down to me. ⁹ If he is able to fight with me and kill me, then we will be your servants. But if I prevail against him and

kill him, then you shall be our servants and serve us."
[10] And the Philistine said, "I defy the armies of Israel
this day; give me a man, that we may fight together."
[11] When Saul and all Israel heard these words of the
Philistine, they were dismayed and greatly afraid." 1
Samuel 17:4-11

David was not having any of these. He knew that he was more
than a conqueror (Roman 8:37) and that greater is He who is in him
than that he who is in the world (1st John 4:4).

Recall another instance in which the children of Israel focused
so much on the physical attributes of their opponents and not the
spiritual. In Numbers 13, Moses sent the 12 spies to spy out the land.
All but 2 brought back discouraging report.

> "Now they departed and came back to Moses and
> Aaron and all the congregation of the children of Israel
> in the Wilderness of Paran, at Kadesh; they brought
> back word to them and to all the congregation, and
> showed them the fruit of the land. [27] Then they told
> him, and said: "We went to the land where you sent
> us. It truly [g]flows with milk and honey, and this *is*
> its fruit. [28] Nevertheless the people who dwell in the
> land *are* strong; the cities *are* fortified *and* very large;
> more over we saw the descendants of Anak there. [29]
> The Amalekites dwell in the land of the South; the
> Hittites, the Jebusites, and the Amorites dwell in the
> mountains; and the Canaanites dwell by the sea and
> along the banks of the Jordan...But the men who

had gone up with him said, "We are not able to go up against the people, for they *are* stronger than we." ³²And they gave the children of Israel a bad report of the land which they had spied out, saying, "The land through which we have gone as spies *is* a land that devours its inhabitants, and all the people whom we saw in it *are* men of *great* stature. ³³There we saw the [h]giants (the descendants of Anak came from the giants); and we were like[i] grasshoppers in our own sight, and so we were in their sight." Numbers 13:26-29; 31-33 NKJV

First of all, these descriptions about the Amalekites is a lie. In Genesis 6:4, we are told "There were giants on the earth in those days, and also afterward, when the sons of God came in to the daughters of men and they bore children to them. Those were the mighty men who were of old, men of renown."

These Nephilim were already on earth before the Noah's flood. They were heroes of the old, men of renown but in God's eyes they were sinners (fallen ones; the meaning of the Hebrew word Nephilim) ...they were strong men who fell. The description of the off springs of Anak were an exaggeration compared to the giants. This exaggeration led them to see themselves as grasshoppers. We should be careful of the types of messages we share with our Christian family about our opponents and how we perceive ourselves in the face of our opponents makes a whole lot difference. Perception can make a whole lot difference between success and failure. Despite this overwhelming negative perception, we thank God for Joshua and Caleb who saw things different and concluded that "Let us go

up at once and take possession, for we are well able to overcome it."
Numbers 13:30 NKJV. Joshua and Caleb "who were among those
who had spied out the land, tore their clothes; and they spoke to
all the congregation of the children of Israel, saying: "The land we
passed through to spy out is an exceedingly good land. If the LORD
DELIGHTS IN US, THEN HE WILL BRING US INTO THIS LAND AND GIVE
IT TO US, 'A LAND WHICH FLOWS WITH MILK AND HONEY.' ONLY
DO NOT REBEL AGAINST THE LORD, NOR FEAR THE PEOPLE OF THE
LAND, FOR THEY are our bread; their protection has departed from
them, and the LORD IS WITH US. DO NOT FEAR THEM." NUMBERS
14:6-9 NKJV

As believers we must be aware that our fights are not physical /
natural things but Spiritual in nature.

> "For we do not wrestle against flesh and blood,
> but against principalities, against powers, against the
> rulers of the darkness of this age, against spiritual
> *hosts* of wickedness in the heavenly *places.*" *Ephesians*
> *6:12 NKJV*

Also, we must not wage our battles as the world does, "For
though we walk in the flesh, we do not war according to the flesh. 4
For the weapons of our warfare *are* not carnal but mighty in God for
pulling down strongholds, 5 casting down arguments and every high
thing that exalts itself against the knowledge of God, bringing every
thought into captivity to the obedience of Christ" 2nd Corinthians
10:3-5 NKJV

While I am not saying that we should spiritualize all our battles,
it is clear that some if not most of the battles we engage in are

spiritual. We will be doing ourselves a disservice fighting such battles in the natural. David was probably a good student of history and also knew that this fight is not a natural fight but a spiritual one that must be fought in the spiritual. Knowing this, ignoring goliath's physical attributes, he boldly declared his battle strategy

> "David said to the Philistine, "You come against me with sword and spear and javelin, but I come against you in the name of the Lord Almighty, the God of the armies of Israel, whom you have defied."
> 1 Samuel 17:45 NIV

David knew this and he also knew exactly where to put his trust. Goliath trusted in his might, his equipment but David trusted in the LORD. He knew that those who put their trust in God shall never be put to shame (Isaiah 49:23, Rom 10:11, Ps 25:3, Isaiah 54:4, Isaiah 45:17, 1st Peter 2:6, 2 Corinthians 10:8). David also knew that "The LORD will cause your enemies who rise against you to be defeated before your face; they shall come out against you one way and flee before you seven ways." Deut. 28:7 NKJV

David as miniature as he was compared to the goliath did not exhibit any fears but rather showed determination and courage; ingredients that are often needed in fighting our goliaths. While goliath was so armed, David was armed with a shepherd's staff, a sling, 5 stones and his steadfast trust in the LORD. I have often wondered why 5 stones. Some think it represent the grace of God. Others think it represents 5 Biblical principles with which you should find your battles

(i) **Faith:** David placed his faith in God: 1ˢᵗ Samuel 17: 37 NKJV "Moreover David said, "The LORD, who delivered me from the paw of the lion and from the paw of the bear, He will deliver me from the hand of this Philistine."

(ii) **Obedience:** The Bible is grounded on obedience. The first sin was committed as a result of failing to be obedient. Obedience to parents is a commandment that comes with a promise. Ephesians 6:1-4 NKJV "Children, obey your parents in the Lord, for this is right. ² "Honor your father and mother," which is the first commandment with promise: ³ "that it may be well with you and you may live long on the earth." And you, fathers, do not provoke your children to wrath, but bring them up in the training and admonition of the Lord." David was very obedient to the parents. 1ˢᵗ Samuel 17:20 "So David rose early in the morning, left the sheep with a keeper, and took *the things* and went as Jesse had commanded him. And he came to the camp as the army was going out to the fight and shouting for the battle."

(iii) **Service:** Christ came to this world to serve and not to be served. Mark 10:45 NKJV "For even the Son of Man did not come to be served, but to serve, and to give His life a ransom for many." David knew of service from the early days. He serves the family by tending the family's flock. When he arrived the battlefield, he asked questions of his brothers and the Israelite soldier as if to suggest they are not living up to their task of serving the nation. He reminded his brother that there is a cause to serve "And David said, "What have I done now? Is there not a cause?" And who refers to himself as a servant said to Saul, ""Let no man's heart fail because of him; your servant will go and fight with this Philistine." David saw his service to the nation as paramount.

(iv) **Prayer**. I recall a song which we were taught in Sunday School and it went like this, "Prayer is the key, prayer is the key, Jesus started with a prayer and ended with a prayer; prayer is the Master key." This Biblical principle cannot be far from the truth. David before facing the goliath prayed in his heart. 1st Samuel 17:45 NKJV "Then David said to the Philistine, "You come to me with a sword, with a spear, and with a javelin. But I come to you in the name of the LORD of hosts, the God of the armies of Israel, whom you have defied." He comes against the goliath "in the name of the LORD of hosts, the God of the armies of Israel" That is a powerful prayer right there.

(v) **Holy Ghost (Spirit)**. In the old testament, the Holy Ghost was present in some people for a specific time and/ or for a specific purpose. The Bible is full of scripture referring to the Spirit of God being with David. 1st Samuel 16:1, 11-13 NIV The LORD said to Samuel, "How long will you mourn for Saul, since I have rejected him as king over Israel? Fill your horn with oil and be on your way; I am sending you to Jesse of Bethlehem. I have chosen one of his sons to be king…So he asked Jesse, "Are these all the sons you have?" "There is still the youngest," Jesse answered. "He is tending the sheep." Samuel said, "Send for him; we will not sit down until he arrives." So he sent for him and had him brought in. He was glowing with health and had a fine appearance and handsome features. Then the LORD SAID, "RISE AND ANOINT HIM; THIS IS THE ONE." So Samuel took the horn of oil and anointed him in the presence of his brothers, and from that day on the Spirit of the LORD CAME POWERFULLY UPON DAVID. SAMUEL THEN WENT TO RAMAH."1ˢᵗ Samuel 18:12 NKJV "Now Saul was afraid of David, because the LORD was with him, but had departed from Saul"

We will need these Spiritual principles to face the many goliaths in lives. These principles are not listed in any order of preference and they are not meant to seen or used independently. But using them alongside each other produces the maximum success results in any battle.

1) What battles are you engaging in right now? Are these battles spiritual or natural?
2) How are you combating or planning to combat these battles (naturally or spiritually)?
3) Where are you putting your trust and why?

List 3 to 5 battles you are trying to battle and defeat in the natural (using your own abilities, knowledge, strength, wisdom etc.)

1) _____
2) _____
3) _____
4) _____
5) _____

Prayer

Gracious Heavenly Father, I pray for your grace. May I use the same grace that fought for David to fight and conquer every goliath in my life. I plead the resurrection power that brought Lazarus and Jesus back to life to conquer all the goliaths that I face now and the future. In Your hand Oh LORD, are power and might that none is able to withstand You. All authority come from You, my fortress. May I surrender all under Your authority, power and control in Jesus Mighty Name. Amen

Chapter Eleven

IT'S THE LORD'S

"Then all this assembly shall know that the Lord does not save with sword and spear; for the battle *is* the Lord's, and He will give you into our hands." 1ˢᵗ Samuel 17:47 NKJV

The battle is not ours; it is the LORD's BUT the VICTORY is YOURS (OURS)

Many Christians today mistakenly live with the notion that they are the ones engaged in the battles we so often face. While it is true that physically we may be the one standing in and facing the challenges of the battles, let it be known that the battle is not ours but the LORD. Knowing whose battle, it is makes the great difference as to how we approach the battle. I know you may not know how to determine if the battle is yours or the LORD's. The simple test I will ask is: whatever you are going through right now, is it as a result of some "stupid and foolish" actions of yours or it is something whose source cannot be easily explained. If your current predicament is as a result of your actions, you can't say that battle is God's. God gave us the spirit of wisdom that we should be able to make wise choices and not get into difficult situations. Let's take a case of a person who constantly spends his or her income on current entertainment and happiness without setting aside any savings for rainy days. When circumstances arise that requires financial resources but because he or she was a stupid or foolish spender, that battles of getting this person out of financial problems are not the LORD's. You could repent from your mistakes and surrender things to God.

When faced with any battles you want to consult with God first. Go to God in prayers. The first step of fighting any battle is spending times on your knee. When you pray and fast about the situation, God may reveal something to you which He may have otherwise not done. In 2nd Chronicles 2, the kings of Ammon, Moab and Mount Seir decided to mount a military campaign against king Jehoshaphat. King Jehoshaphat and his people went before the LORD to seek His counsel and the LORD said this to the king; "Listen, King Jehoshaphat and all who live in Judah and Jerusalem! This is what the LORD says to you: 'Do not be afraid or discouraged because of this vast army. For the battle is not yours, but God's." 2nd Chronicles 20:15 NIV

Understand that the LORD has already conquered all our battles. He reminds us this in John 16:33 NIV by stating "I have told you these things so that in Me, you may have peace. In this world, you will have trouble. But take heart! I have overcome the world." God therefore does not need to defeat the enemy whom He has already defeated even in his (the enemy's) home turf. That victory has been accomplished ("Having disarmed principalities and powers, He made a public spectacle of them, triumphing over them in it." Colossians 2:15 NKJV; also reference Romans 8:37). Given this, we are to fight from the vantage point of victory and not for victory. The LORD calls us therefore to stand and live in victory. In Ephesians 6:10-18, the passage that deals with spiritual warfare and is often quoted by Christians for encouragement, the word "wrestled" is used only once in verse 12 while the word "STAND" is used 4 times in verses 11, 13 and 14.

Recognizing that the battles is the LORD's and the victory is yours, you want to always begin your battles from the vantage point of view of a victor and not a victim. You should be fighting FROM and not for victory. Let's take a close look at two scenarios in the Bible. The first scenario involved the children of Israel making their way into the Promised Land. When God called Joshua, He told them they were going to get a land He (God) has given them Joshua 1:2-3). He did not say go and fight for the land. All the children of Israel needed to do was to show up and the land is theirs. The second case is that of Gideon in Judges 17. Gideon has been called by the LORD to deliver the Israelites from the hands of the Midianites who had been terrorizing them. The LORD first instructed Gideon to reduce his army to 300. The Lord asked Gideon to wake up in the night and go into the camp for He has delivered the enemies into his hands (Judges 7:9). And when Gideon came into the camp, "there was a man telling a dream to his companion. He said, "I have had a dream: To my surprise, a loaf of barley bread tumbled into the camp of Midian; it came to a tent and struck it so that it fell and overturned, and the tent collapsed. Then his companion answered and said, This is nothing else but the sword of Gideon the son of Joash, a man of Israel! Into his hand God has delivered Midian and the whole camp. And so it was, when Gideon heard the telling of the dream and its interpretation, that he worshiped. He returned to the camp of Israel, and said, Arise, for the LORD has delivered the camp of Midian into your hand" Judges 7:13-15 NKJV. Notice how Gideon goes back with great confidence and announces to his troop to "Arise, for the LORD has delivered the camp of Midian into your hand." Gideon was going into the war now knowing that victory has been given and the battle has been fought by the Almighty God. You were created and positioned in a place of victory. Our goal now is to live and stand in that place of victory and not fight for victory. When in a battle, do not be discouraged "for the LORD your God goes with you to fight for you against your enemies to give you victory." Deut. 20:4 NIV

David recognized this truth and went into battle full of confidence, which is why he gladly proclaimed to goliath that "All those gathered here will know that it is not by sword or spear that the Lord saves; for the battle is the Lord's, and He will give all of you into our hands." 1 Samuel 17:47 NIV

Understand that you are already on victory ground and you are operating from such a vantage point because God has given you everything ("Therefore let no man glory in men. For all things are yours." 1st Corinthians 3:21 KJV) and you have been blessed with every spiritual blessing in Christ Jesus as pointed out in Ephesians 1:3 NKJV "Blessed be the God and Father of our Lord Jesus Christ, who has blessed us with every spiritual blessing in the heavenly places in Christ."

You also want to be thankful to the LORD for giving you the victory even though the victory has not yet manifested in the physical. God calls on us to give thanks to Him always (Psalm 150, 1st Thessalonians 5:18, Colossians 3:17). When you give thanks to the LORD, He will bring you honor and you will not be disdained (Jeremiah 30:19)

When I was in the University of ICE, I spent most of my time reminding myself that I am blessed and victorious in Christ Jesus. Each time negative thoughts came up into my mind, I forced myself to think positive and to speak what I was hoping for. It was not easy but I did so many times that positive thinking and speaking became part of me. I recall a day while in Louisiana, we were headed out to the playground. An officer greeted me and that simple greeting led me to witnessing to a brother. That conversation went something like this

Officer: How are you

Me: I am blessed. I hope and pray same for you

Officer: Wow…that is such a good spirit to have. You are in this circumstance and you are still exhibiting a positive attitude.

Me: Do I have a choice? That is my only hope.

One of the detainees who was walking close to me did not find this amusing at all and took it so personal that he had to raise a conversation with me. He began by calling me names (liar) or cautioning me to stop telling a lie. I told him my statement is not in any way far from the truth at all. It was a fact that I am blessed and that such a blessing came because my life is rooted in Jesus. He said to me that I was faking it and that it will just be a matter of days when because of my experiences in that environment that my feelings, attitude and approach will change. Well, he observed me for a couple of days and that attitude did not change. I made it a point that my circumstances will not determine my relationship with God. Regardless of what my circumstance is, God's plan is to bring me through to and into a place of abundance (Psalm 66:12). He wants me to have abundance of peace, joy and an abundance of resources and blessings so that I can be a blessing to others. I was reminded by these verses; "Be anxious for nothing, but in everything by prayer and supplication, with thanksgiving, let your requests be made known to God; [7] and the peace of God, which surpasses all understanding, will guard your hearts and minds through Christ Jesus." Philippians 4:6-7 NKJV. I was in a difficult situation no doubt but I had peace given to me by the Prince of Peace that the ordinary person could not understand. I had hope that was rooted in trusting no one but God. I ceased on this opportunity that God had presented to me and ministered to this brother. I don't know if he accepted Christ that day (I did not present him with the opportunity to make that choice). However, I know I at least planted the seeds in him that day. This brother heard the word. And he knew from our discussion that life is about choices; a choice to be better or a choice to be bitter; a choice to run to the Lord or a choice to run away from Him. I knew that I had either planted the word in him or watered the word that someone had planted. I also knew that one day, someone will either water the word or our God will make it grow (1st Corinthians 3:6-9). Recall that this incident is coming after I am exposed to sun shine and/ or open air for the first time in 17 months of being in seclusion.

1) Do you understand that God has already defeated the enemy in your current battles / challenges?

2) Are you fighting or addressing your battles / challenges from the vantage point of victory or are you fighting for victory?

3) What is your attitude in these battles? Are you a conqueror, victor or do you see yourself as a victim?

List 3 to 5 battles that the LORD fought for and defeated for you

1) _____

2) _____

3) _____

4) _____

5) _____

Prayer

Unchangeable, unstoppable LORD, God, grant me the wisdom, knowledge, and understanding to know that this battle is not mine but Yours. Help me oh LORD to let go and to surrender total control to You. I pray LORD that I will commit this matter into Your Holy and Mighty hands. You, O LORD, the Lion of Judah, make my ways perfect. Thanks for the victory for I know the battle has already been won in Jesus Mighty and infinite name.

Chapter Twelve

HOW I SURVIVED MY DARKEST MOMENTS: MY BIBLICAL AMMUNITION DURING MY BATTLES

During my battles, there are some encouraging Biblical verses that kept me going. These verses provided the "juice" that I needed to keep on. Honestly, there were moments in my battles that I wanted to quit even though I knew that "winners do not quit and quitters do not win." I share some of these verses with you as a guide to come up with your own personal verses. These verses I read them almost every day and some days, I read them many times over. I took Psalm 91 and I personalized it to my situation (see the version below). I also frequently read Psalm 23, 46, 121 …and also the stories of Job, Joseph, Abraham and Hannah. I know the Bible is not just a historical book as many will want to present it. If it is embraced as a Book of Life, it will provide the much needed solutions to all our problems. It is a "Living Book" that breathes and is alive. It is not just a Book. As a matter of fact, he is Jesus. He is the Living Water, the Bread of Life. When you eat or drink (read) of this book, you will never thirst nor hunger. The Bible provided me hope in my despair, strength in my weakness, food in my hunger, water in my thirst, companion in my loneliness, medicine in my sickness just to name these few. Some of the Biblical verses below provided me the much needed hope and positive attitude on daily basis.

1) **Isaiah 45:2-3 NKJV** "I will go before you. And make the crooked places straight; I will break in pieces the gates of bronze. And cut the bars of iron. I will give you the treasures of darkness. And hidden riches of secret places, that you may know that I, the LORD, Who call you by your name, Am the God of Israel."

2) **Isaiah 40:31 NKJV** "But those who wait on the LORD Shall renew their strength; They shall mount up with wings like eagles, they shall run and not be weary, they shall walk and not faint"

3) **Deuteronomy 31:6 NKJV** "Be strong and courageous. Do not be afraid or terrified because of them for the LORD your God goes with you, 'He will never leave you nor forsake you.'" (Also **reference** Deuteronomy 31:8, Joshua 1:5, 1st Kings 8:57, 1st Chronicles 28:20, Psalm 37:28, Psalms 94:14, Isiah 41:17, Isiah 42:16, Hebrews 13:5)

4) **Colossians 3:16** NKJV "There is none like Him and He will not allow His Word to return to Him void."

5) **1st John 4:4** NKJV "You are of God, little children, and have overcome them, because He who is in you is greater than he who is in the world.

6) **Romans 8:31 NKJV** "If God is for us who can be against us."

7) **Psalm 23:4 NKJV** "Yea, though I walk through the valley of the shadow of death, I will fear no evil; for You are with me; Your rod and Your staff, they comfort me."

8) **Psalm 34:17, 19-20 NKJV** "The righteous cry out, and the Lord hears, and delivers them out of all their troubles...Many are the afflictions of the righteous, but the Lord delivers him out of them all. He guards all his bones, not one of them is broken."

9) **Psalm 118:6 NKJV** "The Lord is on my side; I will not fear. What can man do to me?"

10) **Isaiah 50:7 NKJV** "For the Lord God will help me; therefore, I will not be disgraced; therefore, I have set my face like a flint, and I know that I will not be ashamed."

11) **Psalm 9:9 NKJV** "The Lord also will be a refuge for the oppressed, a refuge in times of trouble. And those who know Your name will put their trust in You; for You, Lord, have not forsaken those who seek You."

12) **Psalm 55:22 NKJV** "Cast your burden on the Lord, and He shall sustain you; He shall not permit the righteous to be moved"

13) **Hebrews 10:23 NKJV** "Let us hold fast the confession of our hope without wavering, for He who promised is faithful."

14) **Luke 1:37 NKJV** "For with God nothing will be impossible." (Also reference Luke 18:27, Mt. 9:23, Mt. 19:26)

15) **Mark 9:23 NKJV** "Then Jesus said to him, "If you can believe, all things are possible to him who believes."

16) **Isaiah 54:17 NKJV** "No weapon formed against you shall prosper, and every tongue which rises against you in judgment

you shall condemn. This is the heritage of the servants of the Lord, and their righteousness is from me," says the Lord."

17) **Zechariah 4:6 NKJV** "This is the word of the Lord to Zerubbabel: 'Not by might, nor by power, but by My Spirit,' says the Lord of host."

18) **Psalm 34:10 NKJV** "But those who seek the Lord shall not lack any good thing."

19) **Jeremiah 29:11 NKJV** "For I know the thoughts that I think toward you, says the LORD, thoughts of peace and not of evil, to give you a future and a hope."

20) **Jeremiah 1:5 NKJV** "Before I formed you in the womb I knew you; Before you were born I sanctified you; I ordained you a prophet to the nations."

List 5 to 10 Bible Verses that you have used to see your though challenges

1) _____
2) _____
3) _____
4) _____
5) _____
6) _____
7) _____
8) _____
9) _____
10) _____

Something worth reflecting over

1) It is after the battle field that the path to your palace takes a dramatic turn…It is after David's battle with Goliath that the kid begins his dramatic journey to become king

2) Many of us are willing to fight an army but we are not willing to fight a Goliath

3) Be yourself in fighting your battles. You cannot let someone else fight your battles for you and you cannot take on someone's identity / resources to fight your battles with.

4) When you are in an emergency situation, use whatever you have to fight your battles with. David left the house without the stones but given the emergency, he picked up 5 stones from the Brook, put them in his bag and used them with a sling he had.

5) When you launch at your enemy, you still have resources left for uncertainties (David had 5 stones but actually used 1 leaving him with 4)

6) Your conviction, temperament, determination will mean nothing if you fail to actually act on those convictions

7) There can be no testimony without a test and/ or trial; there can be no resurrection without a crucifixion; there can be

no gain without pain; and there can be no history without a personal story.

8) How will you know He is your ever present help in times of trouble if you have not been in any trouble?

9) Your gifts will always bring you to great places if you make use of them

10) Time is of the essence. We all have 24 hours in a day; 7 days a week. How you use your time will make a difference.

11) At times it is worth fighting for people who despise you. David was fighting for a family who did not like him.

12) A Goliath in front of you is an indication that you are closer to your destiny and/ or breakthrough

Prayer Points

1) Pray that you will always stay alert to recognize that we are constantly in a battle and for our preparedness.

2) Pray for the spirit of obedience (obedience to our Fathers and above all Heavenly Father)

3) Pray that we will always be willing and ready to bring food (bread) to others

4) Pray that we will express our faith, hope and trust in God alone

5) Pray for wisdom and understanding to know that the battle is God's

6) Pray that we will express love for God's people

7) Pray for the Church (the Church with a Capital C) and that there will be a spiritual revival in God's House beginning with you and I.

A Prayer for Mercy with Mediation on the Excellency and Sovereignty of the LORD

Psalm 86 (NKJV).

Bow down Your ear, O LORD, HEAR ME; For I *am* poor and needy. Preserve my [a]life, for I *am* holy; You are my God; Save Your servant who trusts in You! Be merciful to me, O Lord; For I cry to You all day long. Rejoice the soul of Your servant; For to You, O Lord, I lift up my soul. For You, Lord, *are* good, and ready to forgive; And abundant in mercy to all those who call upon You. Give ear, O LORD, TO MY PRAYER; And attend to the voice of my supplications. In the day of my trouble I will call upon You, For You will answer me. Among the gods *there is* none like You, O Lord; Nor *are there any works* like Your works. All nations whom You have made Shall come and worship before You, O Lord, And shall glorify Your name. For You *are* great, and do wondrous things; You alone *are* God. Teach me Your way, O LORD; I will walk in Your truth; Unite my heart to fear Your name. I will praise You, O Lord my God, with all my heart, And I will glorify Your name forevermore. For great *is* Your mercy toward me, And You have delivered my soul from the depths of Sheol. O God, the proud have risen against me, And a mob of violent *men* have sought my life, And have not set You before them. But You, O Lord, *are* a God full of compassion, and gracious, Longsuffering and abundant in mercy and truth. Oh, turn to me, and have mercy on me! Give Your strength to Your servant; And save the son of Your maidservant. Show me a sign for good; That those who hate me may see *it* and be ashamed, Because You, LORD, HAVE HELPED ME AND COMFORTED ME (**in Jesus Might and Matchless Name. Amen**)

Feedback

The Author looks forward to your feedback, testimony, experience or request for prayers so please feel free to reach out at reuel02@gmail.com

Lightning Source UK Ltd.
Milton Keynes UK
UKHW012015060521
383282UK00001B/58